LEADERSHIP
RECONSIDERED

Other Books by Ruth A. Tucker

From Jerusalem to Irian Jaya
Daughters of the Church (with Walter Liefeld)
Private Lives of Pastors' Wives
Guardians of the Great Commission
Christian Speakers Treasury
Another Gospel: Alternative Religions and the New Age Movement
Stories of Faith: Daily Devotionals
Women in the Maze: Questions and Answers on Biblical Equality
Multiple Choices: Making Wise Decisions in a Complicated World
Family Album: Portraits of Family Life through the Centuries
Seasons of Motherhood
Not Ashamed: The Story of Jews for Jesus
Walking Away from Faith
God Talk: Cautions for Those Who Hear the Voice of God
Left Behind in a Megachurch World

LEADERSHIP
RECONSIDERED

Becoming a Person of Influence

RUTH A. TUCKER

BakerBooks

a division of Baker Publishing Group
Grand Rapids, Michigan

© 2008 by Ruth A. Tucker

Published by Baker Books
a division of Baker Publishing Group
P.O. Box 6287, Grand Rapids, MI 49516-6287
www.bakerbooks.com

Printed in the United States of America

Library of Congress Cataloging-in-Publication Data
Tucker, Ruth, 1945–
        Leadership reconsidered : becoming a person of influence / Ruth A. Tucker.
            p.   cm.
        Includes bibliographical references and index.
        ISBN 978-0-8010-6824-9 (pbk.)
        1. Leadership—Religious aspects—Christianity. I. Title.
    BV4597.53.L43T83 2008
    253—dc22   2008033091

To
Dearest Friend
Ann Kelsey
for a living legacy of generosity and compassion
to those in need far and near
through tears and laughter
and
selfless service

CONTENTS

Introduction   9

Part I Critiquing Leadership

1. Leadership 620: Introducing the Topic   15
2. PowerPoint Presentations: Leadership Training Reconsidered   27
3. The Ladder of Success: Capitalism and Competition Reconsidered   39
4. Hitler and Thomas the Tank: Bad Leadership Reconsidered   49
5. God's CEO: Biblical Leadership Reconsidered   59
6. Jesus as Model: Servant Leadership Reconsidered   69
7. Martin Luther King Jr.: The "Great Man" Theory Reconsidered   80
8. Personality and Power: Charismatic Leadership Reconsidered   93
9. Girl Scouts and More: Gender and Leadership Reconsidered   105
10. Where Have All the Followers Gone? Submission and Authority Reconsidered   117
11. President of the Internet: Life without Leaders Reconsidered   131

Part II Creating a Legacy

12. Legacy 620: Bequeathing a Personal Legacy   143
13. Jefferson and Jefferson: Walk Like a Man   154
14. The Lemon Factor: Good from Bad   163
15. An Earthkeeping Legacy: Less Is More   174
16. Smile When I'm Gone: A Legacy of Laughter   185
17. Tender Mercies: A "Cup of Cold Water" Legacy   195
18. Free at Last: Epitaphs and Graveyard Reflections   205

Epilogue   215
Notes   217
Selected Bibliography   227
Index   233

INTRODUCTION

TIME's Person of the Year is not and never has been an honor.
It is not an endorsement. It is not a popularity contest. . . . It is
ultimately about leadership—bold, earth-changing leadership.
Putin is not a boy scout. He is not a democrat in any way that
the West would define it. He is not a paragon of free speech. He
stands, above all, for stability—stability before freedom, stability
before choice, stability in a country that has hardly seen it for a
hundred years. Whether he becomes more like . . . [Stalin] or like
Peter the Great, the historical figure he most admires; whether
he proves to be a reformer or an autocrat who takes Russia back
to an era of repression—this we will know only over the next
decade. . . . [H]e has performed an extraordinary feat of leadership
in imposing stability on a nation that has rarely known it and
brought Russia back to the table of world power. For that reason,
Vladimir Putin is TIME's 2007 Person of the Year.[1]

The understanding of leadership, as *Time* illustrates by
choosing Putin as the 2007 Person of the Year, parallels my own understanding. Whether good or bad, Putin
is above all a leader—a leader with followers. His place at the
table of world affairs owes nothing to popular leadership training forums. Although "he is a believer and often reads from the
Bible," there is no evidence that he has derived his leadership
principles from Scripture. However, when asked what role faith
plays in leadership, he responded: "First and foremost, we should

be governed by common sense. But common sense should be based on moral principles first. And it is not possible today to have morality separated from religious values."[2] Religious values or not, Putin wields power in biblical proportions, and in many respects he could be compared more readily with Moses than could an American president.

Putin's role in stabilizing Russia fits well into the "Great Man" theory. He is a leader for whom power trumps personality. "He is charmless yet adored by his nation. He took a country in chaos and remade it in his own image: tough, aggrieved, defiant."[3] American standards, we must remember, are not the only measures of a "great man." Only time will define his legacy, and then primarily by the Russian people.

In some respects, Putin illustrates a lingering need in the twenty-first century for old-fashioned authoritarian leadership. His effort to bring stability to a vast, unwieldy population requires leadership that is very different from that which is called for in an old and stable constitutional democracy that eschews domineering figureheads. We too easily judge him by our own standards—unless we have glimpsed what Russia was before he came to power. I stayed in Moscow for a week on a research assignment in 1998 when the country was in the midst of a protracted financial crisis. Jobs and savings and social services were in serious jeopardy. The faces in the crowded Underground and on the streets were as cold and gray as were the buildings and landscape and weather. Signs of happiness were almost nonexistent, and as I searched the expressions, I saw far more hopelessness than anger. Enter Vladimir Putin. Today a visitor to Moscow sees color and neon lights and packed eateries—and hope.

Jonathan Steele of the *Guardian* sums up Putin's ongoing legacy:

> What, then, is Putin's legacy? Stability and growth, for starters. After the chaos of the 90s, highlighted by Yeltsin's attack on the Russian parliament with tanks in 1993 and the collapse of almost every bank in 1998, Putin has delivered political calm and a 7% annual rate of growth. Inequalities have increased and many of the new rich are grotesquely crass and cruel, but not all the

10

Kremlin's vast revenues from oil and gas have gone into private pockets or are being hoarded in the government's "stabilisation fund." Enough has gone into modernising schools and hospitals so that people notice a difference. Overall living standards are up. The second Chechen war, the major blight on Putin's record, is almost over.[4]

However one assesses Putin's leadership, it is anything but a contrived fantasy that arises out of institutes and seminars and PowerPoint presentations. How he attained his powerful position of influence is far more in the realm of mystery than in the realm of manufactured programs. To imagine that following steps leading from point A to point B produces a Putin is preposterous.

Imagine instead a world without all the leadership trappings: books and websites and courses and institutes and seminars. What if leadership were not cheap? What if it were something that could not be bought and sold? What if the rewards for leadership had nothing to do with financial gain or prestige? What if what mattered most was legacy? Indeed, apart from a crisis or a critical turn of events, is leadership even necessary?

I will explore these issues in the chapters that follow. They are drawn from two classes I taught on the subject of leadership. Part 1 of the book represents the first time I taught the course, and part 2, the second time—though there is inevitable overlapping.

Part 1 challenges much of the conventional wisdom on leadership. Some of the questions are old and are already largely dismissed as anachronistic in leadership literature; others have never really been asked. Are leaders born rather than made? Is leadership inherently good, or is it really a neutral concept? Is the Bible a guide for leadership? Is Jesus the premier example? Is servant leadership a misnomer? Is the "Great Man" theory of leadership valid? What do personality and charisma have to do with leadership? Are women more suited to leadership roles than men? Is contrived leadership better than no leadership at all? Can leaderless organizations or groups function effectively?

In part 2, we find that the matter of legacy raises a different set of questions that calls us to create more than to critique. We must keep in mind that legacy, no less than leadership, can be contrived. Here we consider legacy in an era of change and how it pertains to ordinary individuals, not just to presidents and popes. We recognize that less is often more and that a seemingly inconsequential act can have a profound effect. We contemplate such diverse topics as laughter and earthkeeping and epitaphs—all with legacy in mind. Along the way we have an eye on calculating our own legacy footprint.

It was not until I began calculating my carbon footprint that I seriously began to recognize how my lifestyle was adversely impacting an already fragile planet. That carbon footprint consciousness prompted me to contemplate my legacy footprint and to wonder what I would leave behind that would be of lasting value.

What we leave behind when we die is a legacy footprint. It is made up of the sum total of good and bad deeds weighed in the balance. This is not a wheelbarrow of works that gets us through the Pearly Gates. It is what is left behind—the footprint of our lives. Christians are so often programmed to think in terms of faith over works—salvation by faith alone. Legacy, however, forces us to think in terms of works over faith. If faith is our ticket to heaven (albeit, oversimplified), works are what we leave behind, the stuff of our legacy—the stuff we hope will rate that seal of approval: *Well done, good and faithful servant.*

Part I

Critiquing Leadership

1

LEADERSHIP 620

Introducing the Topic

It was a warm, sultry August in Grand Rapids, Michigan. I had prepared well for a course I was teaching first time around, Leadership 620. After previewing dozens of books and hundreds of articles, I had chosen two texts and twenty-five articles that I listed on the syllabus as required reading spread out through the short two-week term. The seminary students in my class were all preparing for ministry careers and were eager to gain knowledge on how they might become effective leaders. Although I had never had any formal leadership training myself, I had been teaching and writing in related fields for most of two decades, particularly from a historical perspective. As an introductory course, this was not rocket science. I was a competent teacher, and whatever expertise I lacked I made up for in my teaching style. Parker Palmer was my guide.

The Courage to Teach

In his book *The Courage to Teach*, Palmer challenges teachers to *live* their topics and to be more concerned with the questions than the answers. He counsels the teacher to avoid arrogance and certainty—to "be patient toward all that is unresolved" and to "try to love the contradictions." So I introduced the course with tensions and uncertainties and used Palmer for support as I spoke of the "objectivist myth," quoting him as an authority:

> In the objectivist myth, truth flows from the top down, from experts who are qualified to know truth . . . to amateurs who are qualified only to receive truth. . . . There are only two problems with this myth: it falsely portrays how we know, and it has profoundly deformed the way we educate. . . . In the community of truth, as in real life, truth does not reside primarily in propositions, and education is more than delivering propositions about objects to passive auditors. In the community of truth, knowing and teaching and learning look less like General Motors and more like a town meeting, less like a bureaucracy and more like bedlam.[1]

As a teacher, I love the word *bedlam*. My only regret as I look back on my years of teaching is that I didn't have more bedlam in my classes. But, unfortunately, teachers are forced to teach by the book—by the evaluations. And there is no category for *bedlam*. And if there were, it would no doubt be on the negative side of the ledger, comparable to *disorganized* and *ditzy*. Indeed, there was incredible pressure at the two seminaries where I taught. The pressure, as Jane Tompkins writes in "Pedagogy of the Distressed," was to show "students how smart I was . . . how knowledgeable I was . . . how well prepared I was," rather than "helping students learn what they wanted and needed."[2]

But with the help of Parker Palmer, I resisted the pressure. And during that hot August summer-school course, I emphasized the Palmer pedagogy, insisting that the students should not expect truth to flow from the top down—from an expert who is qualified to know truth. I told them that we would confront far more questions than answers.

Taking a cue from Palmer, I opened up about myself. "Teaching, like any truly human activity, emerges from one's inwardness, for better or worse," he writes. "As I teach, I project the condition of my soul onto my students, my subject, and our way of being together. The entanglements I experience in the classroom are often no more or less than the convolutions of my inner life."[3]

Am I a Leader?

One of the struggles of my soul as I had prepared to teach the course and as I stood in front of my students on the first day of class was an inner voice challenging my qualifications. When I had proposed the course a year earlier, a new administrator and colleague had strongly objected, saying more or less outright that I was utterly unqualified. The members of my division apparently thought otherwise, however, and my proposal passed. But now I was in front of my students and the voice was growing louder. Fortunately, Palmer's voice prevailed. As I had done in the classroom on other occasions, I expressed my insecurities. For many of the students, especially those who had not previously experienced me as a teacher, the self-revelation was no doubt troubling. After all, this school boasted an all-male faculty (except for me), and demonstrating one's expertise in front of the students was the name of the game.

Prompted by a question from Dick, a student whom I had come to appreciate in another class as outspoken and confrontational, I was forced to deal with the matter of whether or not I was a leader, and if not, how could I teach a course on leadership? I was not caught entirely off guard, because I had already mulled the issue over in my mind. But the short answer was *No. I'm not a leader, nor am I qualified.* I quickly caught myself in a free fall and pointed out that bedlam would be our goal. (At least that's how I remember it.) But it was in many ways a good beginning. I had nowhere to go, in the eyes of my students, but to improve.

And as I did, they caught on to the slippery nature of leadership and that they had better love and live the questions since there are no easy answers. My own self-disqualifier alerted them in advance that I had no capability of transforming any of them into an actual leader by the end of the course or even the end of their lives.

But getting back to Dick's question: was I a leader? When I confessed to the class that I was not, I was somewhat apologetic. Some students quickly interjected that of course I was a leader. I was a teacher of the class, a writer, and, I suppose, a just plain decent person. Surely such credentials qualify one as a leader.

In reality, of course, they do not. But then how does one qualify to be a leader? Is a colleague, who dismisses the notions of Parker Palmer and conducts his class with the "truth" flowing from the top down, a leader? If his classroom style resembles that of a General Motors CEO or a bureaucratic chief, does that mean he's a leader?

What we learned in that summer-school class is that the definitions of leadership are infinite, as are the principles and philosophies that accompany the definitions. Throughout the course we developed a solid learning community. The books and articles and video clips and discussion and research projects helped us process the concept and its practical implications in our lives. But the course also created enough tension to make us challenge some basic propositions and to carry with us a healthy supply of skepticism.

Defining the Terms

When defining the concept of leadership, one place to start is Webster's online dictionary. Here the first entry relates to a shoot of a plant or something for guiding fish into a trap. It is the second entry that relates to the subject matter of this book. A leader is obviously "a person who leads." The first three definitions are guide, conductor, and person who directs a military force. Thus, strictly speaking, a leader is someone who actually leads other people—not merely someone who is a *self-identified* leader.

From Webster we move to the definitions offered by those who are well-known in the field. From James MacGregor Burns we are reminded that "leadership is one of the most observed and least understood phenomena on Earth."[4] Malcolm Forbes offers the most basic stock definition: "No one's a leader if there are no followers." Peter Drucker agrees: "The only definition of a leader is someone who has followers." Kenneth Blanchard focuses on influence: "The key to successful leadership today is influence, not authority." John Maxwell is even more confident: "Leadership is influence—nothing more, nothing less."[5]

Such definitions have value when they stimulate discussion and when they simplify the topic. But even with simple definitions, we immediately recognize the contradictions. If leadership is influence, then writers with bestselling novels would be leaders. But where are their followers? So also, a scientist buried in the basement of a computer lab working on the genome project. Many such individuals work very independently and shun the idea of having followers. They are leaders in only the broadest sense of the term.

In his coauthored book *Leadership on the Line*, Ronald Heifetz (founding director of the Center for Public Leadership at Harvard University) opens on page 1 with the sentence, "Every day the opportunity for leadership stands before you." The sentence is followed by bullets with short illustrations. The first bullet is: "A father gets drawn into the same old destructive arguments at the dinner table, but one day breaks out of the pattern and seeks family counseling."[6] But does the act of seeking counseling really qualify as *leadership*? If everything is leadership, then the term becomes meaningless.

Is leadership defined differently if we give it a *Christian* prefix? George Barna defines a Christian leader as someone who "is called by God to lead and possess virtuous character and effectively motivates, mobilizes resources, and directs people toward fulfillment of a jointly embraced vision from God."[7] The spiritual slant sounds good. But *vision from God* is highly subjective. The

19

Bible admonishes us to have a virtuous character; no vision is needed for that. But people differ passionately on their perspectives regarding the will of God. Why is it that so often the will or the voice of God just happens to correspond closely with my own will and voice? Some years ago a large church in Lexington, Kentucky, was divided over whether to stay put in the city or build a megachurch campus on a tract of land out beyond the suburbs. As they evaluated God's will on a matter like this, did they even take into account the environmental impact of driving all the extra miles and the carbon footprint that is required to build a giant structure with acres of parking filled only one day a week? A virtuous leader might very well be able to effectively motivate the majority and mobilize resources to build the new megachurch. But is that really a *vision from God*?

Leadership vs. Management

For some the concept of leadership makes more sense when it is pitted against the concept of management. In an article in the *Harvard Business Review*, Abraham Zaleznik offers a very distinct difference. Leaders can energize a system, even in the midst of chaos, while managers bring stability to the environment. Others have expanded on this comparison: "Leaders are seen as having vision, providing inspiration, giving people purpose, pushing the boundaries, creating change, innovating through others by coaching and building relationships," writes Richard Field. "Managers seek control, follow the rules, set objectives, plan, budget, and get work done through others. They value stability and the use of legitimate power to do the regular work of the organization."[8]

According to Warren Bennis, "Failing organizations are usually over-managed and under-led."[9] Bennis, as the director of a school of leadership and author of several books on the topic, should know. But we ought to be careful about too easily accepting his assessment. Many organizations are failing because a visionary leader has pulled people along with the wrong vision. This is a problem in the church as well as in business. The visionary minister is focused on numbers and buildings and bigger sound systems and elaborate programs. Debts mount, members are disgruntled, and the church of cards collapses. Visionaries are interesting and exciting people, but they carry with them high risk.

The Four Theories of Leadership

According to Ronald Heifetz, there are four general approaches or theories of leadership. The "Great Man" theory gets top billing. "Perhaps the first theory of leadership—and the one that continues to be entrenched in American culture—emerged from the nineteenth-century notion that history is the story of great men and their impact on society." Thomas Carlyle is credited with instilling this perspective in the minds of the general populace through *On Heroes, Hero-Worship, and the Heroic in History*, published in 1841. "Although scientific studies discount the idea," continues Heifetz, "this trait approach [that of examining the personality characteristics of "great men"] continues to set the terms of popular debate."[10]

The second theory Heifetz sets forth is the situationalist theory. "In reaction to the great-man theory of history, *situationalists* argued that history is much more than the effects of these men on their time. Indeed, social theorists like Herbert Spencer (1884) suggested that the times produce the person and not the other way around."[11] Like the "Great Man" theory, this one is not easily examined under a microscope. Thus the current cadre of leadership specialists easily dismiss it.

The contingency theory is merely a combination of the above two theories. "Beginning in the 1950s, theorists began . . . to synthesize the trait approach with the situationalist view," writes Heifetz. "Primary among these synthetic approaches is *contingency theory*, which posits that the appropriate style of leadership is contingent on the requirements of the particular situation. For example, some situations require controlling or autocratic behavior and others participative or democratic behavior."[12]

The fourth theory is the one most often referenced today among leadership experts—the transactional theory. This focuses on the relationship between leaders and followers—"the *transactions* by which an individual gains influence and sustains it over time. The process is based on reciprocity. Leaders not only influence followers but are under their influence as well."[13]

That transactional leadership should prevail over the other three (which ought to be viewed as one) is a very limiting perspective. As cultures are transformed through political and technological changes over the span of time, so does leadership transform. The twenty-first century demands a different type of leader than did the first century. Globalization in recent decades has profoundly altered the concept of leadership, as did democratic and enlightenment ideals in previous centuries. But there are also different stages of leadership that are in progress in any given culture and time frame. This is easily observed in both political and religious realms. America's revolutionary generation, for example, produced a different type of leader than did the following generations. The changing dynamics of leadership in the era during and after the French Revolution is even more striking. The first generation is characterized by vision and enthusiasm and volunteerism and spontaneity while the following generations become more institutionalized. There is a similar pattern in religious movements. Here rules and regulations characterize leadership more than personality and vision. The prophetic voice of the founding leader is replaced by the manager working his way up the ladder of success.

Sixteen Types of Leadership

Leadership seminars frequently promote leadership in generic, abstract concepts, entirely missing the point that there are many different varieties of leadership. The principles of leadership for someone leading a nomadic band of self-sacrificing nuns, for example, might be very different from the principles of leadership for someone developing an innovative software company.

In a slightly different comparison, the leadership principles that apply to a Mother Teresa might not apply to a Bill Gates.

Garry Wills has identified sixteen different types of leadership, based on his definition of leadership as a three-legged stool, the legs being leaders, followers, and goals. "Skills overlap from type to type," he argues, "without obscuring the fact that the military leader's goal is quite different from the social reformer's. A Napoleon's leadership resembles only very distantly an Eleanor Roosevelt's. It's the goal that, in the first place, sets the type. The tactics will be affected, also, by the followers available."[14]

For each type of leader, Wills identifies an individual who exemplifies the type, and also identifies an "antitype." For example, Franklin Roosevelt exemplifies electoral leadership, and Adlai Stevenson is the antitype. Harriet Tubman is named as the radical leader, Eleanor Roosevelt as a reform leader, Napoleon for the chapter on military leadership; King David, for charismatic; Socrates, for intellectual; and Martin Luther King, for rhetorical. Other categories that Wills identifies are diplomatic, business, sports, and artistic. The book is one of the better volumes on leadership, but one might ask, *why only sixteen categories?* There are innumerable fields he did not include, such as environmental, labor union, medicine, and education. The book does, however, illustrate the fact that a military leader is very different from a rhetorical leader.

Twenty Cells of Leadership

If the four theories and the sixteen types of leadership do not comprise enough material for a quiz for session two, I can always add twenty cells. (Fortunately for my students, I don't often administer quizzes—and surely not quizzes calling for memorized lists.) The Leadership Cube is the brainchild of Carter McNamara. "Different people tend to talk about leadership from many different perspectives and not even realize that they are doing so," he writes. "It is very simplistic to generalize about leadership as

23

if the term applies the same way in every situation." He argues that the cube is the key to understanding leadership.

> The Cube includes the following dimensions:
> 1) five domains of leadership
> 2) two contexts of leadership
> 3) two orientations of leadership
> Imagine each of these 3 dimensions along one side of a box, or cube. That would produce a cube with 20 smaller cells (5 times 2 times 2 = 20). Each of the 20 cells represents a unique perspective on leadership.[15]

A unique perspective? Perhaps. But the cube is not so different from other grids used for understanding leadership or life in general. The five domains, for example, are leading yourself, other individuals, other groups, organizations, and communities. When leading oneself, the relevant skills are time management, stress management, and assertiveness. What about money management and continuing education? The items one might add are endless. Although I cannot imagine ever utilizing the cube in my teaching, it does illustrate one of the many ways to carve up the subject matter.

In the end we might ask if *leadership* is for all practical purposes a useless term. McNamara offers some interesting insights about the confusion created by the concept:

> Discussions about leadership today have become so frequent and impassioned, that they have become almost evangelical in tone. . . . We associate any desirable trait to what leaders should be. People exhort others to become better leaders. . . . While this trend has reminded us of the critical importance of leadership and sometimes greatly inspired us on to greater achievements in life and work, it also has diffused the concept of leadership to the extent that the term has become almost useless in really helping people to become more effective in organizations.[16]

But how we define leadership does matter. Dictionaries are critical tools in the world we live in. And that brings us back to Webster's dictionary—and Noah Webster. Was he a leader? Surely not by his own definition that offers illustrations of a guide, a conductor (of an orchestra), or a military office. There is no definition that correlates with someone with vision or influence.

Noah Webster and Leadership

If Noah Webster had written an autobiography, writes Jill Lepore—tongue in cheek—it would have been titled *I Am Not Daniel*. He was often mistaken for Senator Daniel Webster, the "fiery orator" from Massachusetts. Most people who actually knew him found him insufferable. All he cared about was words, words, words. And English dictionaries, after all, were available already—for a price, of course. But Noah was convinced that American English was significantly different from that language spoken across the ocean. If Americans were to be truly independent, they needed their own dictionary.

> On June 4, 1800, Noah Webster, a sometime schoolteacher, failed lawyer, and, staggeringly successful spelling-book author, placed an ad in the back pages of a Connecticut newspaper, just above notices of a sailor's death, a shoe sale, and a farmer's reward for a stray cow. The sailor had drowned; the cheap shoes were "Ladies' Morocco"; the red milch cow had "a white face and large teats." And Webster, who was forty-two, had plans to compile a "Dictionary of the American Language." . . . Seventy thousand entries and a quarter century later, in 1825, he wrote his last definition, much to the relief of his wife and seven children.[17]

The purpose of the ad was to collect some advance orders—rather than controversy. But within days he was mercilessly attacked: "The plain truth is . . . that he means to *make money*." The idea was ludicrous: it is "perfectly absurd to talk of the *American* language. Such a dictionary would be 'at best useless.'" America would be ridiculed for producing "a record of our own imbecility." Imagine including such words as "wigwam" and "caucus" and "lengthy." (What's next, "strengthy"?) Far better to root out these word weeds "than mingling them with flowers." In other words, this *Nue Merrykin Dikshunary* was a "dizkraz."

In the end, we all know that Webster prevailed. Do we credit his success to leadership? Hardly. What saved his dictionary was his very faulty completion schedule that he estimated would take five years, no more than ten. It would consume many chapters in a biography to enumerate all of Webster's setbacks. Moreover, in 1808 he testifies: "A sudden impulse upon my mind arrested me, and subdued my will. I instantly fell on my knees and confessed my sins to God, implored his pardon, and made my vows to him that from that time I would live in entire obedience to his commands." One of the perceived commands was to prove "that all languages derive from a single, original pre-Babel language, the language of Eden." For the next several years work on his dictionary came to a virtual standstill. By 1818, he had not moved beyond the letter *B*.[18]

When the dictionary was published in 1825, most of his harsh critics (including those in the Federalist Party) were dead. Jacksonian Democracy and patriotism held sway. "But what contributed most to the dictionary's success was its timing . . . published at the height of America's greatest religious revival, the Second Great Awakening. . . . Webster's dictionary was a Christian catechism." His "faith shines through on nearly every page." For example: "Meritorious. . . . We rely for salvation on the *meritorious* obedience and sufferings of Christ." Simple words like *love* were illustrated in a Christian context: "The *love* of God is the first duty of man."[19]

For my high school graduation forty-five years ago, I received a brand-new Webster's dictionary. It served me through the years and still sits on a bookshelf today, reminding me how much language has changed in less than a half century. Noah Webster is surely not a model for leadership, but he left a legacy that will continue until the end of time. His motto for his dictionary was a fitting quotation from Samuel Johnson:

> He that wishes to be counted among the benefactors of posterity, must add, by his own toil, to the acquisitions of his ancestors.

2

POWERPOINT PRESENTATIONS

Leadership Training Reconsidered

What is the best way to commemorate the 150th anniversary of a religious denomination—besides throwing a grand party (or worship celebration) at the Van Andel Arena in Grand Rapids, Michigan, and issuing a commemorative book and a new hymn? To some, the answer might be obvious: initiate a leadership institute.

> The purpose of the institute is to help in preparing leaders for service in God's world by coordinating leadership training resources . . . and to supplement such training resources as needed through providing seminars in various places, tutoring, mentoring and encouragement . . . to individuals who are leaders in business, commerce, education, economic and industrial spheres. . . .
> The institute's operations will be funded through the income of a $5,000,000 endowment. The endowment will be raised through special solicitations through church offerings during the anniversary year.[1]

That I would express misgivings about the discretion of my own denomination is fitting. There are surely scores of other denominations and institutions and organizations that I might censure. But it is appropriate that I should be calling my own faith community, the Christian Reformed Church, to account for what I consider its lack of foresight in identifying priorities. Plain and simple, the cult of leadership has conned the Christian Reformed Church.

Replicating Willie Brown

But everybody, it seems, is getting in on leadership training. During recent travel to San Francisco, I spotted a local news headline featuring Willie Brown. The subtitle caught my attention: "Ex-mayor sets up leadership center at alma mater," that being San Francisco State University. Brown ruled as a self-described "Ayatollah of the Assembly" for many of his thirty-one years in the California state legislature, and then served for two terms as mayor of San Francisco. Unlike most who have held such office, he rose to national prominence largely due to his flair and his leadership capabilities as a deal maker.

It would be tempting to label Willie Brown a born leader. He certainly did not have the benefit of training at a leadership center. Yet according to Robert Corrigan, the university president, Brown's story is an important part of the center: "Here you've got a poor kid from a small town in Texas who rose to be a powerful figure in the state of California who also has national presence. That's not a bad role model for inner-city kids who make up a lot of our student population."[2]

Role model, yes. But can one go off to the university to learn how to be a leader like Willie Brown? Or are the students there to learn more about management? The mission of this leadership center "is to train students for careers in municipal, county and regional governments—as political office holders, managers or policy wonks." The focus will be "practical skills in government work at the local level, such as how to mediate a garbage strike."[3]

Here students are learning about real down-and-dirty management struggles—not wide-eyed, lofty visionary goals. But even then, will students be able to follow the leadership of the wheeler-dealer Willie Brown in garbage strike negotiations without the street smarts and charisma and other natural endowments for which he is noted? When it comes to leadership, course work and practical training can only go so far.

Are Leaders Made or Born?

Leaders are *made*, not *born*, so the theory goes. Can leadership be taught? The answer is a resounding *yes* if the thousands of websites and seminar hype are to be believed.

Leaders are made, not born. That is an apt slogan for leadership training institutes. But a *made* leader is not necessarily a leader who has had training per se. In fact, there is little evidence that leadership training, like baseball spring training, actually serves its purpose in training individuals to *be* leaders or to be *better* leaders. In an article entitled "How Can We Train Leaders If We Do Not Know What Leadership Is?" Richard Barker makes some insightful observations. The following abstract sums up his position:

> Views of leadership that focus on the traits and behaviors of the leader are commonly used to develop training programs. Although these leadership training programs have some application, they suffer from several problems. First, there is no reasonable agreement on what traits or behaviors are leadership traits or behaviors. Second, there is no way to differentiate what makes a good leader from what makes an effective manager or an effective person. And third, people who emerge from these training programs rarely become what anyone might define as good leaders.[4]

Individuals who are rightly labeled leaders offer an infinite variety of reasons for their position or role in society. In all the books and articles and websites and personal stories that I have perused on leaders, however, I have never found one example giving credit to a leadership training program or institute (except in the case of a cult leader and his program, such as L. Ron Hubbard and Scientology and Werner Erhard and est, and those were not strictly speaking leadership programs). In many instances these individuals have encountered difficulties in life that have had a significant impact on their leadership style or capabilities. Such trials and errors are often critical in their development. But not PowerPoint presentations and seminars. Leadership simply cannot be taught. Nor can legacy. Legacy institutes and legacy workshops and legacy training programs are simply not a part of our collective consciousness. Nor should they be.

The Selling of Leadership

The big business of management consulting is widely known in the broader world of corporate America, but it captured closer scrutiny in 2007 when regular folks learned that Republican presidential candidate Mitt Romney said in an interview with the *Wall Street Journal* that he as president would "probably" bring in the McKinsey management consulting firm to advise him on reorganizing the government. Under Romney, I ask, would government be streamlined with only two branches or maybe one? "I'm not kidding," he added, for those (like me) who would surely have thought such words were his attempt to bring humor to an otherwise dull interview. But he wasn't kidding, and many people might find such a promise reason enough to support Romney. "If Romney stands for anything, he stands for management consultantship," writes Michael Kinsley. "The myth of the management consultant in general and McKinsey in particular has never been stronger." Kinsley himself was contacted by a McKinsey recruiter years earlier. "What exactly do management consultants do?" he asked. "We provide expertise," the recruiter responded. "But you're thinking of me, and I have no expertise," admitted Kinsley. No problem. "We'll train you."[5]

Reflecting back, Kinsley writes: "Nothing about that interview dissuaded me from the view that consultants spend at least as much energy and brainpower selling themselves to clients as they spend in doing whatever the client pays them to do."[6] Management consulting and leadership training are all under one giant umbrella—all in the business of marketing a product that doesn't exist.

Because leadership training (in all its guises) is a billion-dollar business, it should be put under the scrutiny of proving positive objective outcomes. "Can we really train leadership?" asks Jay Conger, executive director of the Leadership Institute at the University of Southern California, who holds a doctorate in business administration from Harvard Business School and is a leadership training consultant and the author of several books on leadership. The answer, he says, should be an unqualified *yes*. But unfortunately, it is not. The vast majority of the programs are not only shallow but also vastly overpriced. "Companies are not critical enough about how they are designed and what they actually accomplish." They are looking for a quick fix—a magic solution to their lagging profits. "By sending thousands of executives to leadership training programs, they hope that this year's middle manager will turn into next year's Jack Welch." Plato, Conger points out, "argued that he needed 50 years to train a good leader."[7]

Cult of Leadership

Conger's misgivings regarding leadership training are surpassed by those of Bruce Byfield, whose online essays and articles span a wide range of topics. His rant on leadership is as astute as it is provocative. "Business experts always have an air of fantasy about them," he writes, citing "outdated psychology like the Myers-Briggs personality test" and "simplistic hypocrisy like Dale Carnegie's *How to Win Friends and Influence People*." It's a fantasy, he insists, with a deadly serious side: "But while their sense of dislocation fascinates me, business experts can be dangerous and offensive—and never more so than when they are promoting the modern cult of the leader." What is this cult?

31

According to this cult, proving yourself a leader is the way to advance your career. If you are not a natural leader—whatever that means—then you should try to become one by imitating various role models. Some experts go so far to suggest that you should copy the fashion sense and behavior of those higher in the corporate hierarchy. . . . What percentage of people who use these techniques succeed, and what percentage fail? The failure rate must be extremely high, since by definition there are far fewer leadership positions than candidates for them.[8]

"Where do I start," asks Byfield, "explaining what is not only misguided but also deeply insulting about this sales pitch?" A good place to start is to sample some of the numerous online sites. No leadership training program can exist without a website.

Susan Heathfield's Secrets

Susan Heathfield's "Secrets of Leadership Success" is typical. She bills herself as a professional facilitator, speaker, and trainer on topics including interpersonal relationships, organization effectiveness and development, management excellence, marketing services, communication, and leadership. Her impressive list of clients include Michigan State University, Western Michigan University, and Microsoft. And while her "Secrets of Leadership Success" may be a bit off-putting to many academic institutions, her training is based on nothing less than "Transformational Leadership Theory"—whatever that is interpreted to be. But hard science is surely not her forte:

> The first and most important characteristic of a leader is the decision to become a leader. At some point in time, leaders decide that they want to provide others with vision, direct the course of future events and inspire others to success. Leadership requires the individual to practice dominance and take charge. . . . Successful leaders choose to lead. Unlike Keanu Reeves as Neo in 1999's smash hit, *The Matrix*, you get to decide whether you are "the one." The first characteristic of a leader is Choice—leaders choose to lead.

This sort of fantasy is precisely what Byfield is touting in the rampant competitive atmosphere of "proving yourself a leader." But in this case, the *proving* is downgraded to *deciding*. It's a simple matter of choice. Declare yourself a leader, and *voilà!* you are one. The list of characteristics and traits and actions that must identify a successful leader are, as Byfield has characterized such material, "deeply insulting." Here is Heathfield's list:

- Choose to lead.
- Be the person others choose to follow.
- Provide vision for the future.
- Provide inspiration.
- Make other people feel important and appreciated.
- Live your values. Behave ethically.
- Set the pace through your expectations and example.
- Establish an environment of continuous improvement.
- Provide opportunities for people to grow, both personally and professionally.
- Care and act with compassion.[9]

Big Dog

My teaching style easily accommodates students who know more about facets of my topic than I do. When I was teaching Leadership 620, I had a couple of students who, before the class even started, found their niche by becoming online experts on leadership. In the midst of my overview of resources on the first day of class, one blurted out in disbelief, "You've never heard of 'Big Dog'?" I hadn't. I had done some online research, but primarily in search for academic books and articles—ones ideally published by the Kennedy School of Leadership at Harvard Business School. How I missed Big Dog was beyond this student's comprehension. But I quickly made amends, and after the class was over, I spent time with *the* dog of leadership—as it turns out, a major online leadership site.

Harvard Business School is surely not a requirement for one who would be an expert (or self-identified expert) on leadership—nor should it be. Don Clark, who is behind (and in front of) Big Dog, makes no such claims:

> I work in the Information Services/Inventory Control Department at Starbucks Coffee Company's roasting plant in Kent. Prior to that I was Sergeant First Class (E7) in the U.S. Army and retired after 22 years. The first part of my career was in the heavy equipment field (engineers—both combat and construction). My last seven years were at Fort Leonard Wood, Missouri, where I worked as an instructor and then a training developer.

Clark touts his website in grandiose terms, but a case could be made that, as leadership websites go, he has a great deal to offer. He references the *Training Journal*, a British publication, which commends his as "one of the very few worthwhile sites." With a touch of humor, his opening lines set forth his purpose: "Welcome to Big Dog and Little Dog's Bowl of Biscuits! From spanning the globe for great links to cranking out articles, we are hard at work to bring you the finest sites on performance, knowledge, learning, and leadership."[10]

Clark's sections on leadership quotes and leadership links are alone reason to recommend the site. But apart from the wide selections of resources he offers, his perspective is one that is entirely in line with the leadership cult—a perspective summed up in a quote from Theodore Hesburgh, longtime president of the University of Notre Dame: "The very essence of leadership is that you have to have a vision. It's got to be a vision you articulate clearly and forcefully on every occasion."[11] *Vision*, without a doubt, is the most bandied-about term of the leadership cult. No credible leadership guru would discuss the topic without a heavy dose of *vision*.

Big Dog Leadership also offers Clark's own online sixteen-chapter leadership guide. He begins with an overview of "Concepts of Leadership" and discusses "Leadership and Human Behavior." But it is his third chapter, "Leading and Leadership," that clearly establishes his credentials as a guru in the so-called *cult of leadership*:

As a leader, you have to get your people to trust you and be sold on your vision. Using the leadership tools described in this guide and being honest and fair in all you do will provide you with the ammo you need to gain their trust. To sell them on your vision, you need to possess energy and display a positive attitude that is contagious. People want a strong vision of where they are going. No one wants to be stuck in a dead-end company going nowhere . . . or a company headed in the wrong direction. They want to be involved with a winner! And your people are the ones who will get you to that goal. You cannot do it alone![12]

What is this cult of leadership? "The goal is to become some-one that others look up to and admire so that they follow you willingly (that is, are willing to sacrifice their personal time for your business goals)," Bruce Byfield reminds us. "Should you not appreciate this goal, the subtext always seems to be, something is deeply wrong with you (presumably, that you're a natural follower instead)." Byfield's final taunt is a question: "For that matter, who says that people are just looking for a leader to follow?"[13]

Leadership IQ

One of the secrets of getting people to follow the leader—or to buy into a leadership-cult training program—is a clever name. Big Dog obviously has worked for Clark. So also has Leadership IQ, complete with its leadershipiq.com web address. Though the program itself might have been developed by someone with an IQ that doesn't rise above double digits, the name does pique the curiosity of those interested in leadership.

The credentials are imposing. We learn on the opening page of the website that "Leadership IQ has trained more than 100,000 senior executives, managers, and supervisors from the Fortune 500, private enterprises, healthcare, government and non-profit sectors." Unlike other programs, Leadership IQ has no part in the "bland fluff that typically passes for leadership training." Indeed, Leadership IQ is "revolutionizing the science of leadership, and our studies have appeared in *Fortune, Business Week, Forbes, CBS News*, the *Harvard Management Update* and hundreds more."[14]

Like other such programs, this one makes far-reaching promises:

> In this 2-day seminar you'll learn the most successful management techniques from the most admired managers at companies like Disney, Southwest Airlines, GE and Google. . . . This 2-day seminar will transform how you manage people. That's why thousands of companies like Intel, GE, IBM, HP, Citigroup and Johns Hopkins send their leaders to attend.[15]

Who should attend this two-day seminar? the website asks. The shorter list might be who should not attend. In short, virtually everybody: "Managers at all levels, VPs, directors, team leaders, supervisors, and any leader responsible for the daily management of people." Among the things an attendee will learn:

- Build Buy-In for Change
- Coach Employees for Improved Performance
- Manage Low Performers
- How to Speak So Others Will Listen
- The Deadly Sins of Time Management
- Motivate Employees to Go "Above and Beyond"
- Motivate and Inspire Middle Performers
- Influence Without Authority
- Resolve Interpersonal Conflict
- Deliver the Perfect Performance Appraisal
- Retain Your Best Employees
- Manage High Conflict Personalities

If the customer still is not convinced, the site asks: Why Do These Leadership Techniques Work? "They work because they're based on real-life research. This seminar is based on a study of 125,387 managers from 1500+ companies like Amgen, Charles Schwab, Citigroup, DuPont, Hewlett-Packard and more."[16]

Mind Tools

For those who gravitate to a more esoteric way of thinking, Mind Tools may be just the term to capture their attention. It conjures up a spiritual or New Age element that might be lacking in other programs. Indeed, this is not merely a program but a "system"—summed up with the title: "How to Lead: Discover the Leader Within You." It may appear to be a unique take on leadership, but the essential message is the same as that given at any one of the thousands of seminars on how to become a leader:

> Do you want to be a highly effective leader? Do you want to develop the self-confidence, vision, wisdom, motivational impact and delivery skills that the most effective leaders have? And do you want to be the person to whom, quite naturally, other people turn for direction?
> And do you want to learn the leadership "magic" of building a team whose members work together effectively and positively? ... And what about the rewards, respect and personal growth that come with effective leadership? ... [Here] you'll learn the essential, tried-and-tested leadership skills and techniques you need to become a well respected and highly effective leader in business.[17]

The self-endorsements make this program, like the others, seem almost irresistible: "Each year, MindTools.com helps to improve and advance the careers of more than 6,700,000 visitors." Apparently I am one of those visitors whose career has been advanced. By actually enrolling in the program, however, one gets much more. Here is the inevitable leadership list of what one learns to do:

- Create a . . . vision of the future [so] that people will . . . enthusiastically follow your lead.
- Communicate your vision, and see . . . people . . . complete the projects you initiate.
- Grow your self-confidence. . . .

- Build a reputation for expertise [that] your peers will come to respect. . . .
- Make good decisions under pressure. . . .
- Build a strong, flexible and highly effective team. . . .
- Develop the sureness of touch shown by the best leaders. . . .
- Enjoy mutually rewarding, co-operative working relationships. . . .
- Keep people on target and performing well together. . . .
- Learn to inspire and motivate team members so that they'll . . . give their very best.
- Become a truly inspirational leader, and enjoy the perks that come with this.

What does the purchaser of Mind Tools get for her money? "As you learn and start using these skills, you'll become the natural choice for advancement and promotion. Your career will take off, and you'll quickly gather the financial and emotional rewards that come with success. You can join the ranks of the high flyers."[18]

Enrolling in a seminar to learn how to be a leader is as unfeasible as taking a seminar to learn how to teach. There are as many kinds of leaders as there are teachers. Teaching elementary piano lessons, for example, requires a different set of skills than teaching calculus or carpentry or creative writing—all of which require unique teaching proficiencies. If leading refers only to the job of the CEO, then the field narrows significantly, but if leading covers the categories of everything from playground monitor and supermarket produce manager to president and pope, then there is no effective way to teach leadership. Unless training is offered for fields of specialty such as gift-market retailing or marina management, training for leadership is mostly a waste of time.

3

THE LADDER OF SUCCESS

Capitalism and Competition Reconsidered

As I watched *NBC Nightly News* (October 29, 2007), I was intrigued by two opening hooks: a wealthy man speaking out about taxes, complaining that he was paying too little, and another segment on the rapidly increasing number of vice presidents. "Everyone's a vice president," Josh Mankiewicz reported in his satirical tone. The story featured an attractive young Asian woman who barely spoke English, was fresh out of college, and had just been hired by an American firm as a vice president. It sounds impressive. But it's not. It turns out that increasing a title is much more cost effective for companies than increasing a salary. So millions are now climbing the ladder of success as vice presidents. What is the next rung of the ladder for them? President? Hardly. But somewhere above them on the leadership ladder is that prized title of *senior* vice president.

"Oracle of Omaha"

The segment on taxes featured Warren Buffett. He ranks so high on the ladder of success that a title is meaningless. Often referred to as the "Oracle of Omaha," Buffett is most celebrated for his leadership of Berkshire Hathaway, a textile company that he turned around, making it a diversified money-making giant. His attention-grabbing newsworthiness on this particular occasion, however, was his comparing his own income tax assessment with that of his office workers. His percentage (approximately 17 percent of his income) was the lowest in the office, which averaged nearly twice the percentage he paid. With a twinkle in his eye, he issued a challenge to other CEOs to make the same comparison, promising he would donate a million dollars to charity if any of them could show they paid a higher percentage of their income in taxes than on average did their office staff.

Giving a mere million dollars to charity is hardly a risky bet for billionaire Buffett. His estimated net worth is somewhere in the region of fifty billion dollars. Born in the summer of 1930, he was what might be termed a "crash baby." His father was a stockbroker, and he jokes that he was conceived soon after the 1929 stock-market crash when brokering had virtually come to a standstill and his father had little to do.

From his earliest years, Buffett was interested in business. Far from Wall Street, he grew up in the western outpost of Omaha, a Wild West town that became rich by trading its reputation of gunslinging, gambling, and prostitution for railroads and stockyards. Buffett caught the spirit of investment capital from his father. He likes to tell how at age six he bought a six-pack of bottled Coke for a quarter and turned around and sold them for a nickel each, earning him a solid 20 percent return.

Buffett would go on to become the Wall Street wonder, with his story of turning around a "cigar-butt" (one that's failing) company and turning it into one of the world's leading corporations. His turnaround investments are legendary. Buffett's story, like those of Sam Walton and Frederik Meijer (with their strong element of rags-to-riches homespun lore), is part of the American collective consciousness. Indeed, capitalism is as American as baseball, motherhood, and apple pie.

Conspicuous Consumption

As Americans we like to think that we live in a nation that offers everyone an equal opportunity for success and that the competition of capitalism is what has given this country its economic—and democratic—greatness. We concede that nineteenth-century industrialism and banking were conducted by so-called robber barons—most notably Cornelius Vanderbilt, Andrew Carnegie, and John D. Rockefeller—but today we easily think of their charitable foundations rather than their building wealth on the backs of the poor. In fact, some would strongly defend these "Captains of Industry," these leaders of capitalist enterprise. Burton W. Folsom titles his book *The Myth of the Robber Barons*. He and others point out that the cutthroat competition, for example, of "Commodore" Vanderbilt (for whom the term was first used) and his New York Central Railroad actually served to significantly lower rates. "In many ways," writes Warren Meyer, "Vanderbilt was the Southwest Airlines of his day."[1]

Such a comparison is obviously simplistic. The robber barons were living in an era with far less government regulation than today. Workers barely made a living wage, and when they were suddenly put out of work, they had far fewer safety nets. *The Theory of the Leisure Class* by sociologist and economist Thorstein Veblen (1857–1929) is one of the books that I remember well from graduate school. It is a scathing indictment of the lifestyle of these so-called Captains of Industry, especially their "conspicuous consumption" that led to "conspicuous leisure," both of which resulted in "conspicuous waste." But the lifestyle was not confined to the Captains alone. The middle class, and even the poor, sought to emulate this lifestyle. Where would retail advertising be today without conspicuous consumption? The consumer-driven economy depends on it.

For the Omaha-born Buffett, conspicuous consumption has never been an issue. He eats burgers, drinks Cokes, drives his own car, and lives in the Dundee neighborhood of Omaha, and in the same house he purchased in 1958 for $31,500. "There's nothing material I want very much," he shrugs. His self-deprecating humor is endearing: "I buy expensive suits. They just look cheap on me." Like others in his top-of-the-ladder money club, Buffett could buy anything he wants. "If I wanted to, I could hire 10,000 people to do nothing but paint my picture every day for the rest of my life. And the GNP would go up," he drones. "But the utility of the product would be zilch, and I would be keeping those 10,000 people from doing AIDS research, or teaching, or nursing. . . . I'm going to give virtually all of those claim checks to charity when my wife and I die."[2]

Buffett has kept that promise to give away his wealth. In 2006 he announced that he would be giving his considerable fortune to charitable foundations, some thirty billion of it going to the Bill and Melinda Gates Foundation that underwrites various world health projects. It was the largest charitable donation in American history, and, unlike the vast majority of large contributions, it does not have his name attached to it.

Giving away large portions of one's wealth, however, does not alone put one above the rest of the pack in the competitive world of American capitalism, as is demonstrated by the various foundations established in the names of Carnegie, Rockefeller, Vanderbilt, Ford, and others. Buffett, however, does stand above the rest in at least two significant ways. He speaks loudly for transparency. The world of competition and corporate leadership, be it business or education or the church, is hardly known for transparency. I encountered the code of silence myself, when a shabby cover-up was coded with the word "confidentiality." Had the leadership at the institution for which I worked exhibited transparency, bad decisions would not have mushroomed into a monumental debacle.

Leadership Transparency

One of Buffett's well-known quips is: "You can't make a good deal with a bad person." It is a *rule* that goes along with his openness and transparency. He himself has made a strong commitment to integrity and ethical behavior. All CEOs, of course, make such verbal commitments, but he backs up his commitment by, among other things, "disclosing his own mistakes." He is well known in the corporate world for taking steps to clean house. "His criticism of Wall Street fees and compensation of underperforming CEOs, and his pleas for improving corporate governance—all have had a salutary influence on the corporate community." His reputation is supported by quick action: "When Salomon Brothers was embroiled in a scandal with the U.S. Treasury Department," writes Bill George of *US News and World Report*, "Buffett stepped in on a Sunday, took over as chair, installed a new CEO, and saved the firm; he offered federal investigators full disclosure and waived attorney-client privilege, enabling the firm to avoid criminal indictment."[3]

In addition to the matter of transparency, Buffett stands above his corporate colleagues in his understanding of the competitive world of capitalism. I wonder if Veblen might have appreciated his outspoken confessions about wealth and consumerism. As a rich man, Buffett has a rare perspective on money and salaries and worth:

> I personally think that society is responsible for a very significant percentage of what I've earned. If you stick me down in the middle of Bangladesh or Peru or someplace, you find out how much this talent is going to produce in the wrong kind of soil. . . . I work in a market system that happens to reward what I do very well—disproportionately well. Mike Tyson, too. If you can knock a guy out in 10 seconds and earn $10 million. . . . If you can bat 360, this world will pay a lot for that. If you're a marvelous teacher . . . if you are a terrific nurse, this world will not pay a lot for it. Now, am I going to try to come up with some comparable worth system? [No, is his answer.] . . . But I do think that when you're treated enormously well by this market system . . . society has a big claim on that.[4]

The Downside of Competitive Capitalism

Competition, whether in business or in sports, can be a strong force for good in society. But there is the downside as well—when competition becomes a sport in itself. Too often in the game of competition there is not a level playing field. *Level playing field* is an interesting term. It means essentially fair competition, with no advantage shown to either side. The origin of the phrase developed during a time when football and soccer fields were not always level (as they are today), thus potentially giving one team an advantage over another due to the slope—especially if they did not exchange sides of the field. It's relatively easy to level the football field, but in the world of education and business and money-making, there is rarely a level playing field.

A child born into a poor family on the poor side of town will more likely go to a poorer school and get a poorer education than the rich kid on the rich side of town. Give them the same college entrance test. Let them compete. But it's not a level playing field. So also with sports. More and more well-to-do parents, according to a recent news report, are employing sports tutors for their children to give them a competitive edge for college scholarships. For poor children on the other side of the tracks, there's not a level playing field. The same is true with Buffett and his office staff. When it comes to getting ahead, it's not a level playing field when he pays half the percentage of what they pay in income taxes.

Some might imagine that Buffett's own children grew up with every luxury a rich kid could imagine, but that would be far from the truth. "His children," writes Larry Kanter, "have hardly been the typically spoiled scions of the ultra rich." Buffett did agree to help his son Howard in purchasing a farm, but "he told Howie he would . . . rent it to him, requiring his son to fork over a percentage of his farm income and pay the taxes." Daughter Susie was expected to make her own way as well. On one occasion when she was short the twenty dollars to retrieve her car from an airport garage, he insisted she write him a check to cover the cash.[5]

American vs. African Perspectives

I have often asked myself the question, *Is hard-driving competition necessary for leadership success?* In the Western world we seem to think it is. Everything from retail sales and scientific studies to football and fashion is driven by competition. But is there another way? I'll never forget the day my son walked in the door, home for the day from the nearby middle school. He was waving a math test with a 98/100 circled on the top. After a quick expression of pleasure, I asked what kind of grades other kids had gotten. I was subconsciously telling him that a good grade was good only if others got poor grades. Fortunately, I caught myself and turned my attention to his good work, vowing to abandon that kind of competitive negativity.

I've often wondered since then where I acquired such a spirit of competition. Some people and some cultures seem to be devoid of such personal rivalry. I was both surprised and confused when I found the exact opposite of a competitive mentality in my church history class years ago at Moffat College of Bible in Kijabe, Kenya. When I returned quizzes that had a wide span of grades with some high scores and many failures, I noticed a subdued sullenness among all the students—as they routinely looked at each other's scores. But on one day when they all happened to receive high scores, they exhibited an uncontrolled spirit of jubilation. I came to understand that they all considered themselves *members* of the church history class. It was a club of sorts, and as such there was a bonding that knit them together. There was *competition* to do well, but they were competing as a group to reach a high goal. If two or three stood out from the rest, the unity of the group was compromised.

They surely knew the spirit of competition. They played intramural soccer, and there was always a lively rivalry between the two teams. But when they joined as a school to play the hard-hitting team from Rift Valley Academy, their competitive spirit truly came alive. The RVA team, coached by an expert, sported all the necessary gear and was decked out in quality uniforms. Moffat was an older team, including married men, some with half a dozen children. They wore their street clothes and shared the several pairs of sneakers—the sub quickly putting on the shoes of the player coming out of the game. It was not a level playing field. Moffat was the underdog. But the team—or club—spirit of unity among the Moffat players fueled their competitive adrenaline. I had the joy of cheering Moffat on to victory more than once.

I learned a lot from my Moffat students. They taught me, among other things, that competition is not necessary for a lively learning community. I like to think that I taught them the importance of expressing a variety of views and of hammering out differences in an open exchange—even amidst conflict. Parker Palmer speaks perceptively of the difference between competition and conflict in the classroom:

> At its best, the community of truth advances our knowledge through conflict, not competition. Competition is a secretive, zero-sum game played by individuals for private gain; conflict is open and sometimes raucous but always communal, a public encounter in which it is possible for everyone to win by learning and growing. Competition is the antithesis of community, an acid that can dissolve the fabric of relationships. Conflict is the dynamic by which we test ideas in the open, in a communal effort to stretch each other and make better sense of the world.[6]

Women's Reality in a Seminary Classroom

In her book *Women's Reality: An Emerging Female System in a White Male Society*, Anne Wilson Schaef argues that the highly competitive mentality of the Western world is part of a white male system—a system that is not a natural way of life for women (as well as many men) in non-Western cultures. Women, by nature, are less competitive than men, though they quickly adapt to a white male system.

When I presented Schaef's concepts in my most recent leadership class, Rob took issue. This in his mind was typical feminist rhetoric. But I pointed out that in North America—and in most cultures—there has been little opportunity to observe what a female system might look like. That is shown in part by the recent spate of books published on America's *Founding Fathers*. The business tycoons were, likewise, all men—as were the scientists and journalists. Of course, there are exceptions but not enough to seriously challenge the white male system.

I pointed out to my students that this *system* is much closer to home in time and space than the Founding Fathers. We were sitting right in the midst of a white male society—a seminary classroom with male-only décor—more than a dozen large framed photographs of retired professors. Indeed, I was the only woman professor in the school's one-hundred-thirty-year history. I pointedly asked the class if they thought Calvin Theological Seminary might be different today if all the administrators and faculty, but for one, had been female. With Frankie (the only female student in the class) nodding me on, the other students seemed almost confused—wondering what was really the point of my question. I left them to mull it over as I moved on to other matters.

A Noncompetitive System

What might a female system look like? Any such system is already compromised by the dominant operating system. Thus, in any given situation, women often function similarly to men. I well recall the 1984 Olympics when Zola Budd from South Africa was racing against American Mary Decker. Barefoot Budd, whether intentionally or unintentionally, tripped Decker. Decker, enraged, was out of the race, and Budd went on to finish only seventh. No one for a moment doubted their fierce competition.

Compare that tumble with one during a Special Olympics race years ago. When those in the lead suddenly realized their competitors were no longer on their heels, they sensed that something was wrong. As they glanced back, they noticed someone had fallen, causing a pile-up. They slowed down and turned around to help the fallen get up. They were concerned about possible injuries. Once it was determined that there were only skinned knees and no one was badly hurt, the race continued, and the winners were congratulated. Here we have a situation that is outside the white male system. Nothing was lost and much was gained when concern was put ahead of competition.

Could such an attitude ever prevail in big-league competitive sports? Perhaps not. But there is an important lesson about competition to be learned. In recent years, the term *compassionate conservatism* has been touted as the wave of the future, but there has been little substance to support its validity. Here is not the place to coin another phrase, but I do wonder what *compassionate competition* might look like and how that would play out within the context of leadership. Would it recognize a playing field that is not level? Would it say *I'm not paying my fair share of taxes*? Would it go back and help the fallen to their feet before finishing the race?

4

HITLER AND
THOMAS THE TANK

Bad Leadership Reconsidered

The War against Hitler was still in full spate on the day in 1943 when Wilbert Awdry settled down at the bedside of his two-year-old son, Christopher—then ill with the measles—to tell him a story."[1] Here we see the imagination that led to the creation of Thomas the Tank Engine.

Anglican minister Awdry inherited his father's fascination with trains. His father, also an Anglican clergyman, was known by his parishioners as "Railwayman Parson." Awdry had fond recollections of his early childhood after moving to Box, Wiltshire, England, in 1917: "Our house was within sight and sound of the Great Western Railway's main line near Middle Hill. I used to lie in bed at night, listening to the engines struggling up the hill to Box tunnel, and imagining that they were talking to themselves."[2] To the young boy, the trains came alive as they whistled and puffed and as they clanked along the rails.

Awdry was ordained in 1936 and married Margaret Wale in 1938. Soon thereafter their son was born. Christopher was only a toddler when he heard his first Thomas Tank story which was followed by the real thing. "That Christmas," recalls Awdry, "I made Christopher a small, simple wooden model engine out of odds and ends, later christened Thomas." The rest is history:

> Margaret suggested that I "do something" about the stories, and in May 1945 the first book, The Three Railway Engines, was published. Thomas the Tank Engine followed the next year, and new titles followed almost every year until 1972. By then there were 26 books in the Railway Series, none of which, until recently has ever been out of print. I retired from parish work in 1965 and we moved to Gloucestershire, where I went, as I liked to describe it, into "private practice."[3]

Hitler's Train

And what of Hitler? He committed suicide on the eve of publication of the first Thomas Tank book. Though more than two decades older than Awdry, the men were contemporaries. Awdry was ordained a minister and two years later Hitler was inaugurated Führer. Like Awdry, Hitler was also fascinated with trains—so much so that "Hitler's Train" is part of the lore of World War II. His train was the object of many Allied bombing strategies and scenarios with one goal: blow up the train and bury the evil Führer. But the opportunity never came. In the end, April 30, 1945, Hitler took his own life in his bunker. The Allies would not be able to savor the triumph of blasting his train to bits. Five months later, with the war over, General Eisenhower, as military governor of the U.S. Occupation Zone (in the divided Germany) was welcomed to the Hague, aboard Hitler's train. If he couldn't blow it up, Eisenhower apparently reasoned that at least he would enjoy the refinements of Hitler's luxurious train.

Kurt Heilbronn, a GI close to Eisenhower, later reflected on all the modern conveniences:

> [Our cars were driven onto] an automatic ramp. You drove into it, and by pushbuttons it would come out to the platform and you would drive your car on it. It would elevate the car, take it in, turn it around, and park it. . . . The train also had a complete dining car, a car with a kitchen, and it had a complete shortwave car on it that could be used to reach anywhere in the world. This had been used by the German command but was converted for our use. The train also had a running conveyor belt, which, while the train was enroute from one place to another, a meal cooked for a certain general, could then, by a push of a button, have the food delivered to his car. It would automatically stop there, and then, like a desk roll-top, remove the food and serve it. Each general on Hitler's staff had his own particular set of dishes and silverware, and, of course, everything was emblazoned with the swastika. Engraved in the silver, and also done in their crystal glasses, everything was custom made.[4]

Such luxury in trains was unknown to Wilbert Awdry, whose interest in trains was a pastime turned into a livelihood. His name today is barely a footnote in history, overshadowed by his famous creation. Thomas the Tank Engine represented good moral values—the very opposite of what the Führer stood for. And yet, Hitler and Thomas the Tank are both indelibly tied to the topic of *Bad* leadership.

Hitler and Leadership

Was Hitler a leader? Of course he was. It's incomprehensible to me how some so-called experts would imagine that he was not. Only weeks after the death of Hindenburg in 1934, Hitler called for a referendum, seeking approval for his assuming absolute power as both führer and chancellor of Germany. (The word *führer* is German for "leader.") Some 90 percent of the voters gave their approval, stirred in part by a rousing speech days earlier by Rudolf Hess. "I have rarely given a speech as difficult as this one," he began. Why? Because Hitler, according to Hess, was so obviously an exceptional leader that there was nothing more to say.

Hess could be trusted. He knew the man personally: "For fourteen years I have been convinced that he is the only man able to master Germany's fate." He spoke with assurance. "This conviction," he went on to say, "has grown over the years, as the original emotional feeling was surpassed by a solid, documented demonstration." Demonstration of what? Hess had only one answer: "Adolf Hitler's remarkable leadership abilities."

His acquaintance with Hitler began in Sterneckerbrau the summer of 1920. There in a small Munich beer hall "Adolf Hitler, whom I had never heard of, gave a speech to a few dozen people." Here Hess discovered Germany's savior: "His clear, logical and persuasive speech laid out a new political program. . . . He outlined a new Germany from the heart of a front soldier, a Germany that I suddenly realized was the one that had to become reality!" Hess went on to describe the very characteristics of *leadership*:

> This man had driving passion, persuasive logic, and astonishing knowledge. A powerful faith streamed from him—I had never experienced its like. What was most remarkable was that I and the other entirely rational members of the audience did not laugh as he in all seriousness explained that the flag of the new movement for which he and his movement fought would one day fly over the Reichstag, over the Palace of Berlin, indeed over every German building. It would be the victorious symbol of a new, honorable, nationalist and socialist Germany.[5]

Hitler was a leader, and Rudolf Hess was the epitome of a follower. His title was "Deputy Führer," but that was not to be confused with actual power. He "was a shy, insecure man who displayed near religious devotion, fanatical loyalty and absolute blind obedience to Hitler." He was rewarded for his loyalty, but he "was never given any major influence in matters of state due to his lack of understanding of the mechanics of power and his inability to take any action on his own initiative. He was totally and deliberately subservient to his Führer."[6]

Heifetz, Kellerman, and Bad Leadership

Despite Hitler's role in world history, there are those who continue to maintain that he was not a leader. "If we assume that leadership must not only meet the needs of followers but also must elevate them," writes Ronald A. Heifetz, "Hitler . . . does not qualify as a leader. . . . He exercised leadership no more than a charlatan practices medicine when providing fake remedies."[7]

Qualifying leadership in the way Heifetz does is not helpful. It is comparable to saying that all doctors are competent, leaving no place for incompetent doctors except for a charlatan who practices medicine when providing fake remedies. A charlatan is an imposter. He's no doctor at all. Among doctors, there are the competent and the incompetent, the good and the bad. So also with leadership. If we take away the category for bad leaders, we easily blur the line between the good and the bad. By giving the concept of leadership a moral, "value-laden" quality (as Heifetz does), we are less prepared to identify the bad leadership in our midst. If all leaders are good leaders, the same could be said for teachers. To be a teacher is to be a good teacher; a bad teacher is a charlatan. But there are many incompetent, *bad* teachers who are anything but charlatans.

Indeed, it is amazing that the concept of *bad leadership* is not only controversial but also one that is often ignored as it rests on the back burner of leadership discussions. In fact, the case could be made that the most effective *leaders* in the world today (those with the most *followers*) are *bad* leaders. "Any roll call of the world's despots is depressingly long," writes Dale Van Atta. "But only a handful of leaders threaten the security of countries well beyond their borders." In an article titled "World's Most Dangerous Leaders," Van Atta names the heads of state of Venezuela, North Korea, Syria, and Iran. These powerful tyrants ignite followers who are willing to die for what each might term his "vision." And these men are not merely back-alley thugs or hooligans. Bashar Al-Assad of Syria is a London-trained ophthalmologist, and Mahmoud Ahmadinejad of Iran holds a PhD in civil engineering, both having mastered the art of leadership.[8]

Why is there virtual silence on the subject of bad leadership—including bad leadership that engulfs the Christian church? This is not an allusion to those who are less-than-successful church CEOs, those who are failures because their church is not growing—or growing fast enough—by George Barna's statistical standards. The focus here is on bad leaders in our midst. Evangelicals do not have to go across town to point a finger at an abusive priest or at his bishop who is looking the other way. Nor do evangelicals need to point a finger at the money-grubbing televangelists. Bad leaders are only a handshake away. But they are rarely acknowledged unless they are caught with their hands in the collection plate or behind the organ with their pants down.

Barbara Kellerman is the leading expert on bad leadership. In her book by that title, she takes aim at the lack of balance: "But the leadership industry has a problem that years ago I named Hitler's ghost. Here is my concern. If we pretend that there is no elephant and that bad leadership is unrelated to good leadership, if we pretend to know the one without knowing the other, we will in the end distort the enterprise." This, she continues "is misguided, tantamount to a medical school that would claim to teach health while ignoring disease."[9]

Why bad leadership is so routinely ignored in leadership training is indeed mystifying. "In the real world, in everyday life, we come into constant contact," writes Kellerman, "with bad leaders and bad followers doing bad things. In fact, anyone not dwelling in a cave is regularly exposed, if only through the media, to people who exercise power, use authority, and exert influence in ways that are not good." Here she aims her arrows at Christians: "After the recent revelations of wrongdoing by leaders of the Roman Catholic Church . . . so abhorrent it makes us all ill—the idea that some leaders and some followers are bad, and that they might have something in common with good leaders and followers, has not fully penetrated the conversation or the curriculum."[10] Kellerman sees leadership as "a value-free activity—a leader is someone who gets other people to do things he or she wants them to do—whether these things are good or bad."[11]

Where Have All the Leaders Gone?

We see bad leadership all around us in the church and business and politics. In his recent book *Where Have All the Leaders Gone?* Lee Iacocca takes aim at President George W. Bush—particularly in the realm of leadership. Where will Bush rank among the presidents, from bad to good? In polls taken among historians, Lincoln and Washington invariably rank at the top. And who is at the bottom? Typically obscure men who accomplished very little. Rarely has a president been ranked at the bottom for the amount of damage he has done to the country and the world. That may be changing, however. Iacocca might save that space at the bottom for the forty-third president. Having supported and campaigned for him in 2000, Iacocca has become disillusioned and now gives him an *F* in leadership, accusing him of leading the country into war "on a pack of lies."

> Am I the only guy in this country who's fed up with what's happening? Where the hell is our outrage? We should be screaming bloody murder. We've got a gang of clueless bozos steering our ship of state right over a cliff, we've got corporate gangsters stealing us blind, and we can't even clean up after a hurricane much less build a hybrid car. But instead of getting mad, everyone sits around and nods their heads when the politicians say, "Stay the course." . . . Swagger isn't courage. Tough talk isn't courage. Courage in the twenty-first century doesn't mean posturing and bravado. Courage is a commitment to sit down at the negotiating table and talk. . . . Thanks to our first MBA President, we've got the largest deficit in history, Social Security is on life support, and we've run up a half-a-trillion-dollar price tag (so far) in Iraq. And that's just for starters.[12]

There is no doubt that President Bush is a leader—and that he has, despite low poll ratings, thousands if not millions who would still consider themselves followers of his (my diehard Republican in-laws included). But is he a *good* leader? "When we call for leadership in our organizations and politics, we call for something we prize," Heifetz argues. "We cannot talk about a crisis in leadership and then say leadership is value-free."[13] Yes we can. We can talk about a crisis in leadership, in government, in the military, in the teaching profession, because these nouns truly are value-free. What we want is *good* leadership (and government and teaching and soldiering). "Understandably, scholars who have studied 'leadership' have tended to side with the value-free connotation of the term," continues Heifetz, "because it lends itself more easily to analytic reasoning and empirical examination. But this will not do. . . . Rigor in social science does not require that we ignore values. . . . We have to take sides."[14]

Again Heifetz is wrong. The claim that leadership, by definition, is *good* is actually ignoring the very values he touts. We might like to think that all leaders and all teachers and all soldiers and all ministers are good, but by subjecting such terms to solid analysis, we quickly realize that it is not so. Then and only then do we begin to understand what values good *and* bad leaders represent.

The Rest of the Story

So, how does a minister's story told to his sick little boy end up decades later on the bad side of leadership—leadership so bad that the lives of other little children are threatened half a world away? The almost fairytale beginning took on a life of its own as a new book appeared every year until 1972 when Awdry retired. After that, son Christopher took over the book-writing business. "A typical Thomas the Tank Engine story is a little morality play about hubris," writes David Leonhardt. "Almost inevitably, one of the trains tries to run too fast or pull too many boxcars and ends up in a big mess. By the end of the story, though, he comes to understand what he has done wrong." For example, *A Big Day for Thomas* ends with, "Thomas already learned not to make the same mistake again."[15]

By the 1980s, these train stories became a popular children's TV series, and in the decades since, toy Thomas trains have sold by the millions around the world—until it was learned in the spring of 2007 that great quantities of these toys that are manufactured in China owe their bright colors to lead-based paint. Here we see an example of leadership failure—leaders consumed with profit from the production of cheap toys. The company's bottom line trumped the well-being of little children. HIT Entertainment, a company based in England, holds the rights to Thomas and outsources its production to RC2, a toy manufacturing company in China. "Except for a small link on the Thomas Web site to RC2's recall announcement, HIT has acted as if it has nothing to do with the situation."[16]

An appropriate motto for anyone who is claiming to fulfill a leadership role is President Harry Truman's "The Buck Stops Here"—inscribed on a placard on his Oval Office desk (taken from the expression "pass the buck," which means passing the responsibility on to someone else). The very concept of outsourcing is a form of passing the buck, and in the process a once-respected company has lost its most valuable asset—its reputation. This story is "a case study of how not to deal with a crisis" and a case study in bad leadership.

To suggest there are good and bad leaders is, it would seem, so obviously true it needs no defending. Certainly there is a continuum. The leadership of HIT Entertainment is surely not *bad* to the same degree as that of Hitler who ranks on the very bottom of the world's worst dictators. But to try to glorify the word *leader* by denying Hitler the label is counterproductive. If we are to move ahead in our understanding of the word *leadership*, those in the leadership industry must grasp the significance of the bad as well as the good. They are involved in training. If we were to assume that leadership can be taught, they should be concerned about how their training is utilized.

Once it was apparently assumed that anyone who enrolled in a flight school, for example, wanted to learn how to fly an airplane safely. We imagined that they wanted the best training so that once in the air they would not fly into buildings. But 9/11 changed all that. So also with leadership. If leadership can be taught, it can be utilized in the wrong way. Before a university or a religious denomination establishes an institute for leadership, it must think through the very blatant examples of bad leadership. The bad must be studied along with the good.

5

GOD'S CEO

Biblical Leadership Reconsidered

Does the Bible serve as a leadership text? Does God offer a template for leadership? Books and articles in abundance present the twelve steps or seven lessons of leadership found in the Bible. In *The Bible on Leadership*, Lorin Woolfe offers ten leadership imperatives. A reviewer transposed these imperatives into familiar King James language, beginning with: "Thou shalt deal with thine followers with Honesty and Integrity."[1] Fortunately, Woolfe's actual wording is not so lame, but the allusion to the Ten Commandments prompted me to reconsider my own position.

In my previous seminary courses, I simply assumed that the Bible should be gleaned for its teachings on leadership. But I now have serious doubts about using the Bible as a leadership text—or even a leadership guide. I contend that it simply does not in any fashion present imperatives or rules or principles or guidelines for leaders—no more than it presents the imperatives for teachers or chiropractors or public speakers. But if a leader or anyone else is seeking a good set of imperatives, the Ten Commandments are there for the taking. Just imagine a leader who had no gods other than God (including the god of materialism)—a leader who does not lie or steal or envy or commit adultery. These imperatives written on stone by God on Mount Sinai are commandments for everyone, including leaders.

Woolfe maintains that the Bible is the "greatest collection of leadership case studies ever written." No offense to the Bible, but the statement simply is not true. The Bible is not a book of leadership case studies any more than it is an archaeological text or a dictionary of psychological maladies, even though it offers much that may supplement the study of archaeology and psychology. So also with leadership.

That there is a *Leadership Bible* on the market should come as no surprise. We live in an era when there are specialty Bibles for everyone: children, youth, new believers, women, men, family, military, African heritage, Promise Keepers, Spirit Filled (as opposed, presumably, to the Spirit empty), Live Recovery (those struggling with addictions), and many others. So, why not a *Leadership Bible*? For a *leader* in a company like Zondervan— where Bibles reign—such a Bible means profits. Does this Bible actually turn people into leaders or better leaders—apart from the *leader* who came up with the idea?

This Bible is endorsed by John Maxwell, Ken Blanchard, and Richard DeVos of Amway, who states: "*The Leadership Bible* is a great new idea to help all Christians become the leaders we ought to be." Among other things, this Bible promises to "underscore key leadership concepts in every book of the Bible." The general editor is Sid Buzzell, who is listed on the faculty of Colorado Christian University, where he teaches in the school of theology. His "Professional Accomplishments" are stated in the first person: "In the past, I've planted two churches, published two books, and met some wonderful people."[2]

In *The Leadership Bible's* introduction, the editors note that "bookstores today are well-stocked with publications by any number of experts who offer their own philosophy and instruction on dealing with the timeless challenges and opportunities that leaders face." But they insist "this is not one of those books. It is, rather, the Book. . . . In short, this Bible . . . [will] encourage you to develop a leadership style that is based on God's timeless and dynamic Word."[3]

Leadership Bibles

When I began my research for this volume, I naively assumed that there was only one leadership Bible—the one I had often referenced when teaching my course on leadership. But as I was digging further into the topic, I realized I was wrong. *The Leadership Bible* published by Zondervan competes with *The Maxwell Leadership Bible*. The advertising script has consumers in mind:

> This attractive black bonded-leather New King James Version of the Bible (with gilded gold page edges) by John Maxwell [who endorsed the Zondervan *Leadership Bible*], the "leadership expert," takes an in-depth look at God's laws for leaders and leadership. . . . [It] shows us what God's Word has to say about leaders and leadership. It is a Bible resource that explains book-by-book what a godly leader is, what leadership means, what empowering others is about, and how God is glorified when we are all involved in His leadership plan for us.
>
> Articles about the 21 Laws of Leadership in Scripture show us how these Laws are seen in the lives of Bible people. There are also articles about how the 21 Qualities of a Leader are shown in Scripture.[4]

The Leadership Bible, not to be confused with *The Maxwell Leadership Bible*, offers hundreds of biblical role models that readers are encouraged to emulate as they seek to become leaders or improve their leadership skills. The ultimate model presented as one begins the first chapters of Genesis is God. No leadership book has ever topped that standard for a CEO or police chief. Here the biblical principle for leadership is "long-range planning," and God's example is the one to follow:

> Looking ahead into the future, that great unknown, is an integral characteristic of effective leadership. Although as a leader you may not possess a crystal ball to foretell what the future *will* bring, you can and should be planning for what it *may* bring.
>
> God demonstrated his ability to foresee the future in Genesis 3:15. . . . God looked far into the future and saw his glorious victory over all the forces of evil. . . . As the ultimate leader, he made certain that the direction of the history of the human race was headed toward our salvation.
>
> Take some time to discover the direction in which you and those you lead are headed. Where do you see yourself and your team in five years? In ten years?[5]

Because we live in an age of heightened uncertainty, looking into the great unknown is a critical asset of one who is in an important leadership role. The head of Israeli security, for example, is known for his focus on the great unknown, always seeking to anticipate new kinds of terrorist activity (as opposed to American security that develops strategy based on the failed plot by a lone shoe-bomber). Anticipation might well be the first *rule* of leadership—if one is making a list. But to hold an impossible standard out before us and say that we should take a tip from an all-knowing God is both bad theology and ludicrous.

The same could be said in relation to quality control. We also learn from *The Leadership Bible* that one of our skills in leadership should be "Quality/Excellence." This is taught in Genesis 1: "At the end of each day of creation, God says that what he had made was good. . . . God is committed to quality and excellence, since these are expressions of his perfect beauty and Character."[6]

According to *The Leadership Bible*, "a summary of [Jesus's] leadership philosophy can be found in the famous Sermon on the Mount."[7] But that's simply not true. Nowhere—much less in this passage—does Jesus give "a summary of his leadership philosophy"—probably because he didn't have one. We try so desperately to make God—to make Jesus—over in our own image. Many twenty-first-century men (and some women) educated in leadership summits and seminars have leadership philosophies, but not Jesus. He may have had a parable here and there that related to leadership, but a parable is not a philosophy. Like so much of Christian leadership literature that claims to be based on the Bible, this statement is a huge stretch. If the Sermon on the Mount is a "philosophy" at all, it is a philosophy about life, not leadership.

Moses as Leader

As biblical figures go (apart from God and Jesus), Moses is often cited as the greatest leader of them all. Interestingly, New Testament writers focus very little attention on him, in comparison to other Old Testament saints. "Without question, Moses was one of the greatest leaders of world history," so says *The Leadership Bible*. True, he hesitated. But "Like Moses, all leaders will occasionally face tough challenges. . . . At such times they need to follow Moses' lead: Assess the situation, take their fears to God, listen for his response and then obey."[8]

Measured against standard principles of leadership, Moses hardly deserves such accolades. But Moses, in terms of the "Great Man" theory of leadership, has wielded a profound influence in the many generations since his time. This is true particularly in the African-American community where Moses, since the time of slavery, has been more than a mere leader. He is a powerful symbol and an inspirational hero. He demanded of the Pharaoh, "Let my people go!" He led the exodus of God's people from Egypt to the Promised Land. Those words roll off the tongue of the black preacher even today. Moses, lead the way.

The Leadership Bible is subtitled *Leadership Principles from God's Word.* (What more does a hopeful leader need?) "Each book of the Bible begins with its own introduction that underscores the main leadership principles found within." The leadership principle for Nehemiah is typical: "Effective biblical leadership in a context of adversity requires the wisdom and courage that result from radical dependence on God." True, but should one's dependence on God be any less radical in a context without adversity? Under a subtitle, "Benefit," in this same introductory section, the author states that

"Nehemiah also demonstrates that a people's spiritual condition before God is the key to their political and social condition before one another." Such a statement is not necessarily true—not by a long shot. Today there are Christians in many countries whose "spiritual condition before God" is fully as commendable as is the spiritual condition of Americans. But they may live in absolutely dreadful social and political conditions.

Utilizing the Bible as the basis for leadership seminars has become more common in recent years. Lorin Woolfe, the author of *The Bible on Leadership*, has presented thousands of biblically based seminars around the country. The book is subtitled *From Moses to Matthew—Management Lessons for Contemporary Leaders*. "Consider David's courage and innovation in slaying Goliath with just a stone and a sling; Moses' outstanding 'succession planning' in picking Joshua; Joseph and the political skills that brought him to the seat of power. . . . These are leaders among leaders. Their achievements . . . offer a wholly different perspective on business leadership."[9]

If you aspire to leadership, look to Moses or Joshua or David or Daniel, and you will find all the guidance you need to become an effective leader. If they prayed and trusted God and prevailed over their enemies, we should look to them as role models and follow their lead. So it is with much of the Christian leadership literature today. Articles and books—and Bibles—abound. Even if the Bible presents a different and better perspective on leadership, is it truly applicable to the success-oriented focus of business? The example of Paul illustrates the conflict.

The Apostle Paul

The apostle Paul is a key biblical figure who is often cited as an ideal example of a leader. *The Leadership Bible* assumes his leading role—"more than any other single person"—in spreading "the gospel around the world." What application is there for today? "As students of leadership, what can we learn from Paul about broadening and deepening our capacity to shape and build the enterprise we lead?" What made Paul stand out above all others? "Part of the answer is that Paul was so effective because he was so driven."[10] Few people would challenge the claim that Paul was driven, but how effective was he as a leader? Does he model the principles leadership experts are looking for today?

Paul did not assess *leadership* as we do today. His online résumé would have looked very different from that of an aspiring pharmaceutical CEO or megachurch minister that features the common standards of success involving size and status and numbers. Nor does his testimonial read like a success-story promo to kick off a pricey leadership summit at an oceanside resort. Here he is in his own words from 2 Corinthians 11:

> I have worked much harder, been in prison more frequently, been flogged more severely, and been exposed to death again and again. Five times I received from the Jews the forty lashes minus one. Three times I was beaten with rods, once I was stoned, three times I was shipwrecked, I spent a night and a day in the open sea, I have been constantly on the move. I have been in danger from rivers, in danger from bandits, in danger from my own countrymen, in danger from Gentiles; in danger in the city, in danger in the country, in danger at sea; and in danger from false brothers. I have labored and toiled and have often gone without sleep; I have known hunger and thirst and have often gone without food; I have been cold and naked. Besides everything else, I face daily the pressure of my concern for all the churches.

Drawing from both Jesus and Paul, Martin Luther emphasized the theology of the cross, which he contrasts with the theology of glory. The context was the infant Protestant Reformation challenging the powerful and wealthy Roman Catholic Church: "Where the Church recognizes her hopelessness and helplessness she finds the key to her continued existence as the Church of God in the World," he wrote. "In her weakness lies her greatest strength. . . . The theology of the cross is thus a theology of hope for those who despair, then as now, of the seeming weakness and foolishness of the Christian Church."[11]

Luther's words speak volumes to the concepts of leadership today—concepts that do not easily gel with his cross and glory distinctions. Contemporary writers have picked up on that same theme in the writings of Paul. From the passage in 2 Corinthians 11, D. A. Carson challenges the *success* requisite attached to leadership. "It is almost as if the primary (if not the only) incontestable criterion of true apostleship is massive suffering in the service of Christ."[12] Apostleship is the pinnacle of leadership in the New Testament. Suffering is a requisite of that form of leadership because its end is not triumphal success. Its end is the cross.

Was Paul even concerned about the matter of leadership? Apart from the Pastoral Epistles (1 and 2 Timothy and Titus), "it is instructive to notice how little the letters of the New Testament have to say either to or about leaders," writes Dick Tripp. "They are addressed to *all* the Christians in a given place. Paul does include 'the bishops [or overseers] and deacons' together with the rest of the believers, in his opening address to the Christians at Philippi, but then he never refers to them again in the letter."[13]

Churches in Corinth and Rome

Such an omission cannot be explained by arguing that the matter of leadership was being handled properly, and there was no need for Paul's scolding and instruction. Just the opposite. "If ever a church needed strong leadership, it was the church at Corinth, which was beset by division and all kinds of problems," Tripp continues. "Yet Paul's first letter to them is not directed primarily to the leaders, but to the whole community." In chapters 3 and 4, Paul does mention traits for leaders—including serving and stewardship, but the emphasis is on relationships. "He expects the ordinary church members to be mature enough to sort out their own problems and gives plenty of guidelines for doing so." Paul seeks to establish a believing community that is self-sustaining—"where everyone, with whatever gift they may have been given, is a fully functioning member." His emphasis is on "shared responsibility" not with leadership. In Paul's letter to the Romans, the only mention of leadership comes in chapter 12, where he lists it as one of many gifts.[14]

Why doesn't Paul focus more on leadership? Is it because he did not intend for the church to be led by a pope or an archbishop of Canterbury or a megachurch minister? We learn in Sunday school to recite the names of the twelve disciples (though most could hardly be identified as *leaders*). But do we ever memorize the names of the leaders at Corinth or Rome—churches that get a lot of space in the New Testament? Is it because Paul's goal is for a community of believers where "gifted" individuals are involved in shared *leadership*? "Paul's emphasis is on the common or shared responsibility of all for the life of the church, not with the responsibility of leadership."[15]

Leadership today, whether in the church or in the corporation, mimics a pyramid structure in one form or another. There is the senior pastor and various associate pastors and directors and coordinators and on down the line. In the corporation there are CEOs and COOs and senior vice presidents and far too many ordinary vice presidents. In the educational institution, among the faculty, the full professor (perhaps with "distinguished" added to a named title to the professorship) is at the top of the heap, below that associate professor and assistant professor and lecturer. It's all part of the prestige involved in climbing the ladder of success. And Paul would have none of it.

Guidance from the Bible

We do well to avoid using the Bible as a manual for leadership. The span of time and culture between then and now is enormous. Trying to make application between the leadership of Noah faced with a mighty flood and the leadership of Michael Brown (director of FEMA) in the aftermath of Katrina and the flooding of New Orleans is a huge stretch. (Not that this has been done, to my knowledge. But why not, the cynic in me asks, if the Bible is there to give us specific guidance on leadership?)

When it comes to leadership, however, we find the Bible most accessible and practical when we are mining its rich veins for illustrative material rather than hard facts and step-by-step instructions. Gordon MacDonald shows how effectively that can be done. His theme is how the matter of trust relates to leadership: "No biblical leader that I can think of struggled with trust issues more than Moses. Leading a generation of people out of 400 years of slavery must have been like herding cats. Every time the man turned around, someone was questioning his judgment, his veracity, his sense of direction." How did this lack of trust affect him? "You could argue that they finally broke him with their patterns of suspicion and defiance."

It is Paul whom MacDonald identifies as the biblical figure who can teach us the most in this area: "The apostle Paul cashed in on trust when he asked people to give him money to aid in the relief of suffering Christians in Jerusalem. He must have leaned on the trust factor when he convinced Timothy's family to release him to mentorship." It was this same stash of trust that Paul drew on when he "gave strict orders to the Corinthians to discipline a known sinner." Likewise, Paul cashed in on trust when he asked Philemon "to receive a runaway slave back into his home—no longer as a slave but as a brother. No doubt about it: Paul's word in most places was like gold. Trust backed that currency."[16]

How do these biblical figures speak to us today on the matter of leadership—and the matter of trust? Here MacDonald demonstrates how the Bible ought to be used as a guide as he discloses his own failures as a leader:

> I learned quickly in my youngest pastoral years that people would follow only so far if I traded exclusively on my natural gifts: words that came easily, personal charm, new ideas and dreams. . . . The pastor learns the hard way that good ideas and promising strategies are not enough. They can't make it without trust. . . . I once forfeited the trust of people I cared for very much. I lost some very precious friendships. And I lost my honor. To regain any of what was lost took a long time.[17]

6

JESUS AS MODEL

Servant Leadership Reconsidered

Whoever wants to be great among you must be your servant (Mark 10:43). With particular emotion we remember today Mother Teresa, a great servant of the poor, of the Church and of the whole world. Her life is a testimony to the dignity and the privilege of humble service. She had chosen to be not just *the least* but to be *the servant of the least.*

These are the words of Pope John Paul II on World Mission Sunday, October 19, 2003, when he spoke on behalf of this nun of Calcutta, "Foundress of the Missionaries of Charity whom today I have the joy of adding to the Roll of the Blesseds."[1] Few individuals represent servant leadership more profoundly than does Mother Teresa. She took the words of Jesus literally and became a servant to those dying in the streets and to the many who had devoted their lives to following her and following Jesus. Among those who knew her best, she often came across as a snappy, scrappy, single-minded boss, but what she demanded of others she never shirked herself. She was first and foremost a servant.

Does Mother Teresa serve as a model for the secular world? A trendy way to soften the term *leadership* in recent years has been to give it the prefix of *servant*. Such usage is not just confined to the church. Corporate CEOs have bandied around servant leadership for decades. It makes the concept of leadership less authoritarian, with serving others the key ingredient for leading. Jesus is the premier example. As the *rabbi* whom the disciples followed, he washed their feet. Servant leadership. Jesus coined the term. The passage in Matthew is familiar.

The mother of James and John requests a place of honor for her sons in the kingdom. A lot of mothers can no doubt relate to that. But the other disciples were furious, probably wishing they (or their mothers) had thought up the idea first. Here was an opportunity for Jesus to address all of the disciples—and disciples for all generations. He knew that the appetite for *leadership*—for power and authority—was not unique to James and John. To his disciples, Jesus said:

> You know that the rulers of the Gentiles lord it over them, and their high officials exercise authority over them. Not so with you. Instead, whoever wants to become great among you must be your servant, and whoever wants to be first must be your slave—just as the Son of Man did not come to be served, but to serve, and to give his life as a ransom for many.
>
> Matthew 20:25–28 TNIV

On another occasion, Jesus said, "If anyone wants to be first, he must be the very last, and the servant of all." Then he reached out for a child, and said to those in the crowd, "Whoever welcomes one of these little children in my name welcomes me" (Mark 9:35, 37). And again he said, "I tell you the truth, unless you change and become like little children, you will never enter the kingdom of heaven. Therefore whoever humbles himself like this child is the greatest in the kingdom of heaven" (Matt. 18:3–4). Those are sobering words, and we dare not play fast and loose with them in any discussion of leadership.

Servant Leadership Defined

It is interesting that Jesus is not even mentioned in the opening-paragraph description of "Servant Leadership" in the online encyclopedia, Wikipedia:

Servant leadership is an approach to leadership development, coined and defined by Robert Greenleaf and advanced by several authors such as Stephen Covey, Peter Block, Peter Senge, Max De Pree, Margaret Wheatley, Ken Blanchard, and others. Servant leadership emphasizes the leader's role as *steward* of the resources (human, financial and otherwise) provided by the organization. It encourages leaders to serve others while staying focused on achieving results in line with the organization's values and integrity.[2]

The article goes on to point out that the concept of servant leadership is as ancient as Chanakya (or Kautilya), an important thinker from India, who wrote about the concept in his fourth-century BC book, *Arthashastra*:

"the king [leader] shall consider as good, not what pleases himself but what pleases his subjects [followers]"

"the king [leader] is a paid servant and enjoys the resources of the state together with the people"[3]

Wikipedia is an encyclopedia with an international and interreligious scope. Citing Hindu literature is appropriate. But Christianity also has its servant kings—most notably Good King Wenceslas.

Good King Wenceslas

Shrouded in legend, Wenceslas is the patron saint of the Czech Republic—a saint for whom a multitude of churches and a square in Prague are named. But most of us know him from the delightful Christmas carol that is too infrequently sung. Here we find this servant king leading the way through the blizzard when he might have sent the page alone on this mission of goodwill:

> Good King Wenceslas looked out
> On the feast of Stephen,
> When the snow lay round about
> Deep and crisp and even.
> Brightly shone the moon that night
> Though the frost was cruel,
> When a poor man came in sight
> Gath'ring winter fuel.

The king learns from his page that the poor man lives leagues away "underneath the mountain . . . against the forest." They secure food, wine, and firewood and trudge off through the snow and "bitter weather." When the page "can go no longer," the king tells him to walk in his footsteps. The last verse powerfully depicts servant leadership.

> In his master's steps he trod
> Where the snow lay dinted.
> Heat was in the very sod
> Which the Saint had printed.
> Therefore, Christian men, be sure
> Wealth or rank possessing,
> Ye who now will bless the poor
> Shall yourselves find blessing.

On the Wikipedia site, Jesus follows the reference to Indian literature, with a quotation from Mark 10:42–45, a parallel passage to that quoted above from Matthew. The distinction is then made between servant leadership and a more traditional style:

Unlike leadership approaches with a top-down hierarchical style, Servant Leadership instead emphasizes collaboration, trust, empathy, and the ethical use of power. At heart, the individual is a servant first, making the conscious decision to lead in order to better serve others, not to increase their own power. The objective is to enhance the growth of individuals in the organization and increase teamwork and personal involvement.[4]

Robert K. Greenleaf

Robert K. Greenleaf (1904–1990) is the most frequently cited expert on servant leadership. As an executive at AT&T in the 1960s, he observed that one of the primary reasons for the unrest among youth was because American institutions—including institutions of higher education—were not serving them, and the public in general, well. The problem was one of leadership. The solution was transforming leadership into servant leadership: "The servant-leader is servant first. . . . It begins with the natural feeling that one wants to serve, to serve first. Then conscious choice brings one to aspire to lead. . . . The difference manifests itself in the care taken by the servant—first to make sure that other people's highest priority needs are being served."

So influential is Greenleaf that there are now leadership programs named for him, including the Greenleaf Center for Servant-Leadership, a leadership academy at my alma mater, Baylor University, that draws on his teaching—emphasizing that *servant* comes chronologically before *leader*. In illustrating the concept, Frank Shuskok states that Mother Teresa, for example, was no doubt a leader. Did she prepare to be a leader or become a leader because of her desire to serve first?[5] But is Baylor's academy or any other leadership institute or program really going to find a leader who is a servant? And if so, is that servant actually going to be able to pass this philosophy of leadership along, and how would we know if this is truly servant leadership?

Can servant leadership be measured? Greenleaf sets forth criteria for his now classic test:

> Do those served grow as persons; do they, while being served, become healthier, wiser, freer, more autonomous, more likely themselves to become servants? And what is the effect on the least privileged in society; will they benefit, or, at least will they not be further deprived?[6]

But is an affirmative response enough to qualify one as a true servant leader? Or must there be a lifestyle component? Greenleaf's test certainly does not rise to the example of his role model and hero, Leo.

Leo as Leader

So, to whom do we look when contemplating the ultimate role model for servant leadership? What is the first name that comes to mind? *Jeeez-US*, with the accent on the second syllable, pitching up to a question mark—as kids schooled in children's church would answer on cue. But as the Wikipedia article suggests, Jesus is not the only one in the running. Nor is Mother Teresa. Leo holds an important spot at the top. And not Leo the Great, who is sometimes given the rank of first pope of the Roman Catholic Church (by ones who don't give the apostle Peter that position). Popes are supposed to be servants, but with all their finery and pomp and ritual they are not easily confused with those who wait tables or clean the floors.

This Leo is a key pilgrim in Hermann Hesse's novel *The Journey to the East*. He is the epitome of servant leadership, the one who inspired Greenleaf to write "Essentials of Servant Leadership" and *Servant Leadership*.

The Journey to the East combines flights of fantasy with routine events, as the League (a secret society) journeys through space and time. For example, in Zurich they come upon Noah's ark. The destination is the East, symbolically the "home of the Light," a place with the promise of spiritual renewal. The pilgrims include such historic figures as Plato, Pythagoras, Mozart, and Albertus Magnus, but the main character turns out to be Leo, a humble, good-natured, menial servant, who does the chores with song rather than grumbling.

All goes well in a spirit of happy harmony among the pilgrims—until the party comes to a mountainous gorge, Morbio Inferiore, where Leo disappears. The spirit of unity quickly ruptures as fear and anxiety degenerate into anger and blame. Discord ensues until the group disintegrates, each one going his separate way. At the end of the story, the narrator (who was one of the pilgrims) has an opportunity to join the order that sponsored the League's journey. When he appears before the High Throne, he is shocked to find that Leo is the president. He all along has been the true leader disguised as a servant. Or, is he the true leader in plain sight?

The story has a good moral, but it is pure fiction. True, there are servant leaders among us, the Mother Teresas of this world. But the claim of *servant leadership* in established organizations is most often at its best an expression of ingratiating nicely, and at its worst a façade—just plain phoniness.

Everyone likes to see the CEO donning an apron and serving the baked beans at the company picnic. But don't imagine for a moment that such is servant leadership. When she takes a big salary cut to save jobs, only then is the concept of servant leadership beginning to bud. Servants are low-paid menial workers, or they're volunteers. The megachurch preacher or the seminary president living in a mansion dare not claim anything resembling servant leadership. Servant leadership is lifestyle transformation. Anything less is phony.

Aaron Feuerstein

Is it possible to be a CEO servant leader? I was struck several years ago when I watched a *60 Minutes* segment on a 1995 raging, wind-whipped conflagration that destroyed Malden Mills in Lawrence, Massachusetts—a company known worldwide for its Polartec products. Lawrence, due to much of its manufacturing sector moving overseas and south of the border, was already struggling with high unemployment. Now, two weeks before Christmas, more than two thousand people would be out of work. What was stopping the mill owner and president, Aaron Feuerstein, from collecting the insurance money and retire? His family had owned the business for decades, and he was now in his seventies.

But Feuerstein was a "man of his word" and a God-fearing Jew. The day after the fire, he called in all employees for a meeting and promised to keep them on the payroll as long as money was available. His plan was that they would all return to work in a new state-of-the-art manufacturing plant. The employees were teary-eyed and grateful—but not surprised. He was well known by his employees to be a good man.

> From the time he took over the company in 1957, Feuerstein became an active player in the community. He extended credit to struggling local businesses, sponsored English classes for immigrant employees, and offered training for textile workers. He took special care of his own workers, making sure they had a safe and comfortable work environment and paying higher wages than most of his competitors. Even union leaders praised him, calling him "a man of his word" and "extremely compassionate." One union official said, "He believes in the process of collective bargaining and he believes that if you pay people a fair amount of money, and give them good benefits to take care of their families, they will produce for you."[7]

When interviewed on *60 Minutes* and asked why he had contributed his own money to pay the employees and rebuild the company, he answered in a somewhat bemused tone, "What else am I supposed to do with the money?" He and his wife had all the material wealth they needed for happiness—a modest condo and lots of books. He explained how his Jewish tradition directed his course of action: "When all is moral chaos, this is the time for you to be a *mensch*" (a Yiddish term for someone whose compassion goes above and beyond what justice demands).[8]

President Clinton recognized him in a State of the Union address, and accolades came from all over the world—though he dismissed such recognition. What he did, he insisted, should not be the exception but the rule.

Despite his sacrifice for the company—and his *servant leadership*—there is no fairy-tale ending for Malden Mills. After several years of struggle following the fire, the company went into bankruptcy. Feuerstein's endeavors fell short of the mark. He was forced to step aside as president, and in 2004, the restructured company replaced him with a new CEO. Yet his name will forever be linked with decent and compassionate leadership.

Here is a Jewish businessman setting an example that is rarely seen in Christian ministry. Indeed, where in the landscape of twenty-first-century Christianity do we find the *servant leader*? Truly there are exceptions and they deserve to be heralded. But in most instances such people are obscure Lone Rangers who are making a difference one step at a time.

Despite such high standards as those set by Jesus and Mother Teresa and Leo and Feuerstein, the concept of servant leadership continues to be promoted as something one can simply learn to do by reading a book or taking a course or attending a seminar—or by simply pronouncing oneself a servant leader. "I am a servant leader," said Kathryn Ballou, the new dean of nursing at Graceland University in a recent interview. "I try to be transparent; there is very little I keep from my faculty. When we share as much information as humanly possible, we are bonded together." Roy Tanner, seeking a seat in the US Senate from Florida, promises voters: "I'll bring principled servant-leadership to the US Senate, I will accept no special interest funding and pledge to serve only a single term."[9]

Even if the academic dean and the political candidate are now or in the future fulfilling their claims, do those claims in any stretch of the imagination rise to the standard of servant leadership?

John Woolman

In *Servant Leadership*, Robert Greenleaf cites the example of John Woolman, a true leader. He was a Quaker, growing up in Pennsylvania in the early eighteenth century. His story begins in his journal, now a literary classic. Without that journal we would not know about his "conversion." He was just a boy given to doing the kinds of things boys often do—in this case throwing rocks at a robin's nest occupied by baby robins just hatched.

Mother robin was protective, and young John nailed her with a rock, felling her to the ground. "At first I was pleased with the exploit," he confessed, "but after a few minutes was seized with horror at having, in a sportive way, killed an innocent creature while she was careful for her young." That moment was a turning point in his life.[10]

A turning point, yes, but other forms of "youthful vanities" occupied his time. Temptations continued to beset him during his teenage years, but he held fast to the Bible and to the Quaker meetinghouse. Then in his twenties, Woolman heard the voice of God that would set him on a *servant leadership* path—a voice of God not, as we so often hear of today, telling one to move across country for a big pay raise and promotion. The voice he heard would set him on an anti-slavery course: "I had many fresh and heavenly openings, in respect to the care and providence of the Almighty over his creatures in general, and over man as the most noble amongst those which are visible." The heavenly openings came from Scripture. From Ezekiel, he read of the duty of being God's "watchman"—recognizing that God was calling him to be the watchman for slaves.[11]

The opportunity came quickly: "My employer, having a negro woman, sold her, and desired me to write a bill of sale."[12] He obeyed, but it was an incident that would set him on a course of turning the Society of Friends into an anti-slavery movement. That Quakers were opposed to slavery from the beginning is a common misunderstanding. Indeed, "many of the eighteenth-century American Quakers were affluent, conservative slave holders." For the next three decades—until the time of his death at age fifty-two—Woolman devoted his life largely to anti-slavery activities.[13]

Unlike many other later abolitionists, Woolman was no firebrand.

> His method was unique. He didn't raise a big storm about it or start a protest movement. His method was one of gentle but clear and persistent persuasion.
> Although John Woolman was not a strong man physically, he accomplished his mission by journeys up and down the East

Coast by foot or horseback visiting slave holders. . . . The approach was not to censure. . . . Rather his approach was to raise questions. What does the owning of slaves do to you as a moral person? What kind of an institution are you binding over to your children? Person by person, inch by inch, by persistently returning and revisiting and pressing his gentle arguments over a period of thirty years, the scourge of slavery was eliminated from this Society, the first religious group in America formally to denounce and forbid slavery among its members.[14]

In addition to personal conversations, Woolman wrote "epistles" and other essays, and he addressed meetinghouses and the yearly meetings of the Friends. His primary focus was on slavery, but he was also concerned about the treatment of Native Americans and took up other humanitarian causes as well.

For those who would aspire to *servant leadership* today, John Woolman is a remarkable role model—a man of self-sacrifice, sensitivity, and perseverance.

7

MARTIN LUTHER KING JR.

The "Great Man" Theory Reconsidered

In the minds of many contemporary leadership experts, the "Great Man" theory is dated. It's not exactly flat-earth science, these experts contend, but it is misleading. The "Great Man" harks back to a world of mythology where giants, knights, and kings ruled and where maidens were as vulnerable as they were beautiful. These superheroes of legend offer little to the understanding of leadership—especially a leadership that is learned from books and PowerPoint presentations.

But though relegated to the amateurish level of "popular" social science, this theory simply will not go away. It may be one of those ideas where common sense reigns in spite of all the scholarly evidence to the contrary. Leadership training is big business—business that is wholly dependent on proving that leadership comes from learning, not from innate traits and life experiences. Apart from the inherent conflict of interest, there are other reasons not to trust the experts. The "Great Man" theory should not even be categorized as theory. It is so obviously true that its simplicity gets in the way of those who theorize. We know the truth of it by observation and instinct.

I illustrate this proposition by citing two Republican two-term presidents. I like to think I stand outside political partiality in this case because I voted for neither of them. Nor would I vote for either of them if I had the chance to do it over again. The first, Ronald Reagan. He was a leader of "Great Man" stature. His force of personality and his determination of will left a profound legacy of conservatism that lives on—for good or for ill. His leadership came from the deep well of who he was as an individual. It's patently silly to imagine President Reagan going to three-day seminars and studying leadership theories on his way to the White House.

The second two-term president I cite is George W. Bush. He is not a leader of "Great Man" stature. He will not leave a legacy of conservatism that will bring anything other than shame. Is there any leadership course or any leadership expert who could have taught him to become a good leader? My answer would be the words of former University of Indiana Coach Bobby Knight, when he was speaking to a university class of business students: "The first thing you people need to know about leadership is that most of you simply don't have it in you."

If you're a conservative politically, you proudly acknowledge Ronald Reagan as a "Great Man." George W. Bush is someone you may continue to defend but in your heart you know he will never meet your expectations. A footnote to this proposition is that Reagan's closest contemporary in the "Great Man" arena was Prime Minister Margaret Thatcher—the Iron Lady.

History and the Great Man

Perhaps my affinity for the "Great Man" theory is prompted by my love of history. My academic degrees, my writing, and much of my teaching have merged through the discipline of history. And the skeleton that holds the body of history together more than anything else is the succession of great men—and women. Ralph

Waldo Emerson asserted that there is "properly no history, only biography." History as a discipline is the history of people. There are wars and documents and organizations and architecture and art, but never without people. Geology, archaeology, and zoology relate to history, but they are not history proper.

There are many what-ifs in history that point to the great man. I often ponder these counterfactuals in the field of church history. *What if* Constantine had not been converted to Christianity and extended toleration to fourth-century believers? This counterfactual goes far beyond the field of church history. It profoundly affects the history of the world. *What if* Charles Martel had been defeated by the Islamic forces in 732 at the Battle of Tours? Would most of the world be Muslim today? *What if* Martin Luther had shrunk back in the face of threats and the Reformation had never gotten off the ground? *What if* John Calvin had remained a Catholic and stayed in France? Calvinism spread to England and Scotland where Puritanism was exported to the New World— changing the face of American history.

To ignore the "Great Man" theory is to dismiss the twists and turns of history. From Socrates and Shakespeare to Florence Nightingale and Nelson Mandela, the stories of nature and nurture that formed these individuals are as fascinating as impossible to reproduce. There simply are no duplicates, and so much the better. While such ambiguity and imprecision frustrates those who would offer ten principles or twelve steps or demand analytical breakdowns, it leaves the door wide open for those who are truly visionary. To be inspired by a great man or woman opens vistas of opportunity. To follow the programmed contents presented by a workshop instructor stifles creativity and vision.

Yet biography as history is dismissed—largely because science has sought to usurp history. "With the rise of the behavioral sciences, however, the Great Man Theory has fallen out of favor," writes David Cawthon. "Instead, scholars have directed their focus elsewhere, and for the past 50 years behavioral theories, contingency theories, and characteristic analyses ad infinitum have dominated the literature." But he goes on to argue that "despite having accumulated a plethora of data, we have failed to penetrate the mystery" of leadership. Yet most current leadership experts scoff at the "Great Man" theory. "Warren Bennis and Burt Nanus (1986) consider the proposition that leaders are born, not made to be myth. They note that leadership is a learned skill and has little to do with natural forces."[1] Their words represent the perspective widely held in the leadership industry:

> Biographies of great leaders sometimes read as if they had entered the world with an extraordinary genetic endowment, that somehow their future leadership role was preordained. Don't believe it. The truth is that major capacities and competencies of leadership can be learned, and we are all educable, at least if the basic desire to learn is there and we do not suffer from learning disorders. Furthermore, whatever natural endowments we bring to the role of leadership, they can be enhanced; nurture is far more important than nature in determining who becomes a successful leader.[2]

Churchill as Great Man

Despite the leadership industry's attempt to kill off the "Great Man," the theory is still alive and well—even in an assortment of leadership training venues. Winston Churchill, for example, lives on in a website, appropriately found at www.winston-churchill-leadership.com. Referencing the site itself, the opening question is: "What is Winston Churchill Leadership?" The answer succinctly summarizes what the reader should expect:

> When Britain stood alone in May 1940 the greatest Englishman of the 20th century took up the leadership of his country. This site seeks to define Winston Churchill's leadership. We shall explore his leadership principles as well as the man himself, his hobbies (painting and cigars), those famous Churchill speeches, his enormous wit and a collection of the best Churchill quotes.

The rationale purports to be practical. Ian Chamberlain, who hosts the website, introduces himself as "a Leadership, Management and Sales Training Consultant" who has found in Churchill the ultimate great man: "The debt owed by the Free World to Sir Winston Churchill remains immeasurable. His legacy is all around us." Chamberlain's task is to serve his clients—"some of the world's finest multinational companies" that seek his expertise "to develop the leadership skills of their young ambitious middle managers." These companies are looking for "the latest, cutting edge skills to keep them ahead of their competitors." So how does Churchill fit into this equation? He is the model whose "leadership principles" are foundational for training ambitious middle managers to be the leaders of the twenty-first century.[3]

But like all great men, Churchill had his problems with leadership—a point that the website fails to highlight. In an Associated Press article entitled "Papers Show Churchill's Cabinet Battles," Thomas Wagner writes that "the aging British prime minister threatened to quit in 1954 in order to quell a revolt by Cabinet ministers, angered at his high-handed leadership style." The issue was the hydrogen bomb:

> He argued that the H-bomb was "essential" to deterring a Soviet attack. "[We] must be able to make it clear to Russia that they can't stop effective retaliation. That is (the) only sure foundation for peace," he said. Harold MacMillan, then Britain's housing and local government minister, was appalled. It was, he said, a "shock to be told, casually, that we were going to do this." . . . In 1954, Churchill got into even more trouble with his Cabinet when ministers learned he had sent a secret telegram to Soviet Foreign Minister Vyacheslav Molotov, proposing a grand Anglo-Russian summit in Vienna, Austria. The ministers were outraged he had not consulted them first.[4]

Is this what leadership ought to be? And should this great man inspire leadership training programs? Is taking decisive action without consultation appropriate leadership? In many ways this style worked for Churchill, but to offer such an example to ambitious middle managers makes little sense—apart from explaining that the great man is not something that arises out of leadership training workshops.[5]

The Great Man as Model

Nevertheless, we love the stories of the great men and continue to study their lives for lessons on leadership and various other disciplines. "Thomas Carlyle crystallized this view in his 1841 volume *On Heroes, Hero-Worship, and the Heroic in History*," writes Ronald Heifetz. "Although various scientific studies discount the idea, this *trait approach* continues to set the terms of popular debate. . . . Based on this view, trait theorists since Carlyle have examined the personality characteristics of 'great men.'" Leadership, according to this theory, is based primarily on a variety of learned skills and innate talents and capabilities.[6]

As long as there are institutes and schools and conferences and seminars on leadership, there will be a focus on the "Great Man." It is difficult to promote the concept of leadership without actual examples. And as gender conscious as society has become, leadership is still very much a man's world. Without the "Great Man," leadership theory would be just theory. I have used the Harvard-published Heifetz text, *Leadership Without Easy Answers*, for my leadership course lecture preparations. At the time, I assumed it was a great text because it was *scholarly*. But I deleted much of that material the second time I taught the course, in part because of what I perceived to be contrived *leadership theory*. Chapter 9, "Modulating the Provocation," for example, begins with the following paragraph:

> The principles of leadership that we have discussed—identifying the adaptive challenge, keeping distress within a productive range, directing attention to ripening issues and not diversions, giving the work back to the people, and protecting voices of leadership in the community—apply to leaders with or without authority. However, because the benefits and constraints differ, those who lead without authority must adopt strategies and tactics that are at once more bold and subtle.[7]

Whether the "Great Man" is dismissed in favor of social science or used as the basis for emulation, the great man himself continues to rise up in every generation and change the course of history.

Martin Luther King Jr.

To illustrate what he is trying to say about leaders without authority, Heifetz picks a "Great Man," none other than Martin Luther King Jr. King's *leadership* before and after Selma is dissected to make sense of Heifetz's theory, rather than allowing King to illustrate the jumble and mixed bag of what leadership and legacy have come to mean. Heifetz is very critical of "the common personalistic orientation to the term leadership, with its assumption that 'leaders are born and not made,'" charging that it "is quite dangerous. It fosters both self-delusion and irresponsibility."[8] With all his flaws, it is difficult to argue against the fact that King rose up in a crisis (*situationist* theory of leadership) to become a "Great Man" leader. Analyzing his story by way of leadership theory easily distorts King's spur-of-the-moment decision making and minimizes the significance of his character and personality.

Through Heifetz's eyes, even after Selma, King did not have "the informal authority to provide the necessary holding environment and direct [his followers] productively. . . . [H]is success and survival depended on his own sensitivity to the severity of the stress he generated and the pace at which he did so." Furthermore, "his interventions had to take into account the level of distress the larger system would withstand."[9]

Was King really conscious of "modulating the provocation"? I seriously doubt it. King, by all accounts, had intuition more than he had analytical understanding of "the level of distress of the larger system." And nowhere does Heifetz quote King in letters or notes indicating that "he and his strategists would have to monitor the level of distress they would generate. . . . But at the national level, they would have to keep the distress within the proper range—above the threshold for stimulating public and political engagement." Heifetz continues to thrust his own terminology on King four decades after the fact; for example, having King monitoring "President Johnson's responses [that] would indicate how well the public at large could tolerate the adaptive challenge issuing from Selma."[10] In actuality, King and those around him were in most cases flying by the seat of their pants. King was in the right place at the right time.

King is a great case study in leadership and legacy, but there's no indication that he was in any stretch of the imagination a leadership theorist in the mode of Harvard professor Ronald Heifetz, who serves as King Hussein Bin Talal Senior Lecturer in Public Leadership and Founder of the Center for Public Leadership.

Daddy King

Actually, King's knack for leadership is far more interesting than Heifetz suggests, and his teacher—also his father—was a practical man, not a theorist. Indeed, his father Mike King, the son of a drunken sharecropper, was the ultimate practitioner:

> A near illiterate, he was determined to break into Morehouse College and to become a refined pastor. At age twenty-one he was a fifth-grader in a remedial school in Atlanta. For several years he served a tiny church in Atlanta called Traveler's Rest where he labored with a reading ability "barely beyond a rank beginner" and preached to deacons who "didn't know the alphabet. A member of the lowest caste of rural Negroes (his schoolmates had taunted him unmercifully for smelling like a mule), he set his cap to marry the princess of Ebenezer, the boss's daughter, Alberta Williams. A poor man with dung on his boots, he dreamed of living in a brick house with a fine porch and shutters on the windows."[11]

Marrying the preacher's daughter set the stage for Mike King to succeed his father-in-law—a transition that took place in 1931. It was a poor, struggling church (with a respectable attendance of four hundred) that rose in attendance to some four thousand by 1940—spurred on by the often dictatorial and always calculated and shrewd leadership of the young Mike King. Almost immediately he began consolidating the finances of the various church auxiliaries so as to have more direct control over expenditures. In order to increase giving, he implemented a system of publicizing "each member's contributions—amounts plus names." He "also established birth-month clubs whose members engaged in friendly fund-raising competitions to the benefit of the whole congregation." But he did not stop at merely shaming people into giving or coaxing them through competition.

> King's shrewdest financial maneuver he learned from the successful insurance companies on Auburn Avenue. Because their clients were not able to afford large policies, insurance salesmen collected small premiums on a monthly or even weekly basis. King recruited the insurance people as members who in effect became collection agents for the church. The salesmen acquired a new field of customers, and the church benefited in many ways from a new system that not only increased contributions, but also created a network for communication and home care.[12]

For Mike King, leadership was instinct more than education, practice more than theory. And for him, the "Great Man" theory of leadership proved to be decisive. A critical turning point during this period of church growth for Ebenezer Baptist was a sabbatical excursion to Europe, Africa, and the Holy Land that the church gave him in 1934. In Germany, inspired by the legacy of Martin Luther, he decided to legally change his name and that of his five-year-old son from Michael to Martin. If a mere monk could change the course of religious history, so also could an up-and-coming black preacher in Atlanta. From that point on Martin Luther was forever attached to King's own legacy.

Church growth did not initially come without conflict. But "if Mike King had his critics, they were soon silenced by the church's dramatic financial recovery as well as the irrefutable passion with which he willed one thing: the advancement of Ebenezer. Whether by Machiavellian business instincts or blunt-edged buffoonery, Mike King got his way."[13]

Rhetorical Leadership

Heifetz misses the critical essentials that made Martin Luther King Jr. an extraordinary leader. A more practical—more usable—reflection from the standpoint of leadership is that of Garry Wills, who identifies King uniquely as a "rhetorical leader." Wills focuses on the importance of heritage and role models. From a child, he was "destined to be a fourth-generation preacher." His maternal grandfather had seen promise in his father, Mike King, "this stubborn plodder" who "twice flunked introductory English" at Morehouse College (where he was finally "accepted because of his father-in-law's influence"). With rhetorical genes and the blood of preachers running through his veins, Martin Luther King Jr. had the foundation for greatness. "The entire discipline of these men's lives issued in the eloquence they kept refining for pulpit use." The future belonged to him.[14]

King, like few before and after him, was a true leader—though it was leadership he did not seek. "Like many prophets in the Bible," writes Wills, "King did not aspire to the kind of leadership he finally undertook. He would gladly have fled the task, like Jonah. But the task pursued him." He was not a man of heroics and great courage. "Reluctant to go to jail, he was shamed into going there after so many young people responded to his speeches and found themselves in danger."[15]

In many respects King was not even the *visionary* that leadership gurus insist is a necessary requisite. He borrowed his ideas—and his rhetoric—from others. Indeed, his most famous lines were borrowed. More than a decade before King's "I Have a Dream" speech, Archibald Carey, another black preacher, had called people to action with virtually the same words that King later borrowed: "From every mountainside, let freedom ring. Not only from the Green Mountains of Vermont . . . but from the Ozarks . . . from the Stone Mountains . . . from the Blue Ridge . . . from every mountainside, let freedom ring."[16]

This speech, according to Wills, was "the greatest American speech given since Lincoln's time." And Lincoln's presence was very real. The Lincoln Memorial was the backdrop, and King picked up Lincoln's "Four score and seven years ago" with his own "fivescore years" since Lincoln's Gettysburg Address. King's fivescore becomes a refrain: "One hundred years later. . . . One hundred years later, the Negro is still anguished. . . . One hundred years later. . . ." Lincoln had issued the Emancipation Proclamation, but one hundred years later African Americans were still not free. King was calling for that promise to be fulfilled: "*Now is the time* to make real the promises of democracy. *Now is the time* to rise from the dark and desolate valley of segregation to the sunlit path of racial justice." Here King shines brightly as a rhetorical leader.

King's role in the civil rights movement does not easily fit into the categories of leadership theory. He was pushed—or pulled—into a leadership role, aided by inherited rhetorical skills as well as numerous seminary and doctoral preaching courses. He was not a trained leader, and any attempt to replicate him today through leadership training programs would be doomed to failure.

King's Legacy

King fits the now-dismissed "Great Man" theory of leadership, if for no other reason than the fact that his name is so frequently called forth to illustrate a great leader. But more than his leadership per se is his legacy—a legacy that, despite his flaws and failures, rises out of his Christian faith. He confessed that his faith was often as weak as his courage. This was true after he spent a night in the Montgomery city jail (for going five miles over the speed limit). If he could have chosen a place of renown in the annals of American history, it would have been as a great scholar or preacher. Surely not the leader of a crusade against the Klan and the white southern establishment. He knew too well the dangers—the lynchings—facing uppity black men.

As he sat with a cup of coffee at the kitchen table, long after Coretta and his little girl had fallen asleep, he was pondering the previous night. Perhaps, as he looked at Coretta, he was also reminded of his wedding night in Alabama. With no accommodations open to African Americans, he and his bride slept at a funeral home belonging to family friends. But on this night, as his memories far and near cluttered his mind, he sensed God speaking to him—as he later recalled in a sermon:

> And I sat at that table thinking about that little girl and thinking about the fact that she could be taken away from me any minute. And I started thinking about a dedicated, devoted and loyal wife, who was over there asleep. . . . And I got to the point that I couldn't take it anymore. I was weak. . . . And I discovered then that religion had to become real to me, and I had to know God for myself. And I bowed down over that cup of coffee. I will never forget it. . . . I prayed a prayer, and I prayed out loud that night. I said, "Lord, I'm down here trying to do what's right. I think I'm right. I think the cause that we represent is right. But Lord, I must confess that I'm weak now. I'm faltering. I'm losing my courage." . . . And it seemed at that moment that I could hear an inner voice saying to me, "Martin Luther, stand up for righteousness. Stand up for justice. Stand up for truth. And lo I will be with you, even until the end of the world."[17]

Here King is coming to grips with his legacy. No amount of graduate training or seminars on leadership could have prepared him to follow the voice of the Lord.

From Racist to Civil Rights Advocate

King's legacy is far greater than a holiday in his honor—or the countless schools and parks and streets named for him. His life transformed a nation and turned racists into civil rights advocates. Philip Yancey is a case in point. Born in 1949 in Atlanta, the hometown of Martin Luther King Jr., Yancey's neighborhood was a world away. Had they actually been together on the same bus, King would have been expected to sit in the back and give up his seat if a white person wanted it. Although Yancey's own family was very poor and lived in low-rent housing and trailer parks, they were white and thus considered themselves higher on the status scale than the King family. "We ate in different restaurants, played in different parks, and attended different schools and churches," Yancey recalls. "Our governor called for the Georgia Tech football team to forfeit their Sugar Bowl game invitation in 1955 when he learned that the opposing team, Pittsburgh, had a black player on its reserve squad." It was not uncommon to see signs that read "No dogs or Coloreds allowed." Lester Maddox was a religious role model—Maddox of fried-chicken-restaurant fame who, with ax handles and a .32 caliber pistol, kept blacks from dining. "The Ku Klux Klan had an almost mystical hold on our imagination," Yancey recalls. "I wrote school papers about it. It was an invisible army, we were taught, a last line of defense to preserve the Christian unity of the South."[18]

Today, Yancey speaks with conviction against racism. Unlike his northern white counterparts whose racism is less conscious and more disguised, he has *been there, done that*, so to speak. His words are powerful—especially to a broad evangelical audience that remains suspicious of King and his cause. Yancey makes no effort to turn King into a sanctimonious saint. Indeed, he recognizes King's failures in his placing him alongside those re-counted for their faith in Hebrews 11—flawed *leaders* such as Noah, Abraham, Jacob, Rahab, Samson, and David.

> I certainly once dismissed him. Yet now I can hardly read a page from King's life, or a paragraph from his speeches, without sensing the centrality of his Christian conviction. I own a collection of his sermon tapes, and every time I listen to them I am swept up in the sheer power of his gospel-based message, delivered with an eloquence that has never been matched.[19]

There is no doubt that King was a great rhetorical leader. A whole generation and more were "swept up in the sheer power" of his spoken words. But it is King's legacy more than his hesitant leadership that places him in the "well-done" category before God. His legacy is far more than his monumental role in civil rights legislation. His legacy is also captured in his role in changing the heart and mind of a once poor little racist white boy.

8

PERSONALITY AND POWER

Charismatic Leadership Reconsidered

The upside of charismatic leadership is that in the short run it can be very effective, encouraging staff and others to buy into future vision and potential change in an organization," so says Marshall Young, a fellow of strategic leadership at Oxford University's prestigious business school. The downside is "the danger that charismatic leaders become dangerously egotistical and convinced of their own omnipotence."[1]

A well-known example of charismatic leadership in recent decades is Lee Iacocca. How well I remember back in the 1980s when his name and face were everywhere in the media as he pitched his autobiography, *Iacocca*. In fact, he paved the way for the era of bestselling business biographies and business books generally. But do you really want an Iacocca running your business? Jim Collins, who has ridden the Iacocca wave with his own bestselling business books, including *Good to Great*, does not think so. Collins argues that what is really needed in business is the "triumph of humility" as is demonstrated by the truly great leaders. He points to Iacocca as a very capable—and egocentric—leader whose highly acclaimed success is short-lived. Iacocca's stunning coup at Chrysler—turning around an automaker that was on the skids—was a celebrated triumph. But was his business savvy only a flash in the pan? Collins seems to suggest it was:

> The auto maker's stock rose 2.9 times higher than the general market about halfway through his tenure, but then Iacocca diverted attention to transforming himself. He regularly appeared on talk shows, starred in 80 commercials, entertained the idea of running for president of the United States and promoted the autobiography which sold 7m copies. Iacocca's personal stock soared but Chrysler's stock fell 31% below the market.[2]

David Cole, director of the Center for Automotive Research at the University of Michigan, agrees, pointing to harsh criticism of Iacocca, particularly related to his failed effort (with Kirk Kerkorkian) to take control of Chrysler again in the 1990s.[3]

Identifying the Leadership Personality

What does personality have to do with leadership? Is a charismatic personality a plus or a minus? Are there certain kinds of *leadership* personalities? Historically the leader was often equated with a strongman—the hard-nosed authoritarian who ended up at the top in the game of "king of the hill." That is particularly true of American leadership. They were the Founding Fathers, the lawmen, the cavalry officer, Robber Barons, the John Waynes of the West—mostly men who had worked their way up in life. The boss is tough, and we associate him with rugged individualism, with manliness, with the frontier spirit, with innovation and inventiveness. This was the kind of leadership that was not schooled in three-day training seminars and institutes named for big contributors.

Does a charismatic personality aid in the aspiration for leadership? In recent decades, a charismatic personality often seems like the prime requisite whether in the church or business or politics. The Nixon-Kennedy presidential debate of 1960 was a landmark. From that point on no candidate could dismiss the profound implications of personality and charisma. Today, looking back nearly a half century at the debate, Kennedy seems hardly polished. In office, Kennedy, with Jackie at his side, exuded charm and sophistication as the Camelot president.

Television personalities in recent years have set a standard that is coming to be expected in politics and other professions. Even the news reporters are expected to look and act charming. Not so in the days of Walter Cronkite, the grandfatherly figure everyone trusted. Imagine him starring on *Saturday Night Live*, as did *NBC Nightly News* anchor Brian Williams in November of 2007. Williams has the kind of charisma and charm that is more and more considered necessary for successful leadership.

"Without question, the key word in leadership is charisma (charisma: charm, personality, appeal, magnetism, natural leadership)," says Eli Harari, who bills himself as the Thinking Coach. "There are definite qualities expressed through charismatic leadership that need to be learned and developed before being successfully applied in leadership roles. . . . Astonishingly people-handling skills and strategic thinking skills account for 90% of what a leader needs today and only 10% are required technical skills."[4]

From Character to Charisma

It's interesting to study leadership from a historical perspective—even from the short history of the United States. The earliest leaders, whether Puritan fathers of the Massachusetts Bay Colony or the revolutionary founders of a new nation, were not known for their charisma. Apart from Ben Franklin, they would be totally out of place among contemporary charismatic politicians exemplified by Bill Clinton. Indeed, political and business leaders have historically placed little worth on charm and smoothness.

"But shortly after World War I the basic view of success shifted from the Character Ethic to what we might call the Personality

Ethic," writes Stephen Covey. "Success became more a function of personality, of public image, of attitudes and behaviors, skills and techniques, that lubricate the process of human interaction." The Personality Ethic was marked by the explosion of what became known as PMA (positive mental attitude). Norman Vincent Peale, with his hugely successful volume, *The Power of Positive Thinking*, stands out. Positive thinking was the key to power—to leadership. Transform yourself through optimistic thoughts and then infuse your company with your contagious positive mental attitude. The concept was expressed in pithy maxims such as "Your attitude determines your altitude" (your height on the ladder of success), "Smiling wins more friends than frowning," and "Whatever the mind of man can conceive and believe it can achieve."[5]

The Personality Ethic was also seen in human and public relations techniques, which, according to Covey, are "clearly manipulative, even deceptive, encouraging people to use techniques to get other people to like them, or to fake interest in the hobbies of others to get out of them what they wanted, or to use the 'power look,' to intimidate their way through life." He concedes that "some of this literature acknowledged character as an ingredient of success, but tended to compartmentalize it rather than recognize it as foundational and catalytic."[6]

Today the game has evolved into a soft enterprise of what some might call leadership for sissies. It is no longer presented as a bullying game of "king of the hill." There is more hand-holding than shoving, more negotiating than commanding. The words tossed around today would be foreign to the John Wayne rough-and-tumble lawless frontier where men were men. Only a sissy would be seen standing around a table piled high with hors d'oeuvres, dressed in *GQ* Friday casual, talking about synergy.

Dale Carnegie, Guru of Ingratiation

But personality and charm in the field of leadership are not new. Dale Carnegie was the king of currying favor—the guru of ingratiation. He should not be confused with the famous Andrew

Carnegie (though he hoped he might be) who made his fortune in steel and many other ventures, now remembered largely for his philanthropy. Born Dale Carnegey, he changed his name early in his career, hoping to draw on the name association with this widely respected (and unrelated) American icon.

Dale Carnegie (1888–1955) is known primarily for *How to Win Friends and Influence People*, which remained on the *New York Times* bestseller list for some ten years, now having sold more than fifteen million copies. The course based on the book continues to be taught today more than a half century after the death of the author. In fact, one of my seminary students (now a minister in South Dakota) swore by the course, insisting that teaching it to the seminary community could transform the institution.

Carnegie was born and raised on a poor Missouri farm where he learned the value of hard work, rising at four in the morning to do the milking. But farming was not for him. Nor was school teaching, although he attended a nearby teachers' college. He became a salesman, peddling everything from correspondence courses to bacon and soap. His success in selling won him accolades and awards.

But his dream for success lay in the related field of communication, especially his aspiration to become a Chautauqua lecturer. The early twentieth century was an era when the traveling lecturer was a celebrated public figure—recognized for knowledge and communication skills. But along the way to becoming a lecturer, he veered down the path of acting, a career that ended soon after his debut in *Polly of the Circus*, a traveling road show. Out of money and down on his luck, he found cheap lodging at a New York City YMCA. Here he came up with the idea of teaching classes on public speaking, giving the YMCA 20 percent of his take for the use of their space. From this modest beginning in 1912, the Dale Carnegie course evolved, and a quarter century later, in 1937, the book for which he became known was published.

How to Win Friends and Influence People does not have the term *leadership* in the title, but it is clearly written with that in mind. It has four major sections, each of which includes a list of core principles. The first section, "Fundamental Techniques in Handling

People," has three core principles, the third of which illustrates the technique of manipulative leadership: "Get the other person to do what you want them to by arousing their desires."

The second section begins the series of lists. I recently heard a publisher say that list articles and books sell well, whether "Ten New Looks for the New Year" or "Seven Ways to Save Money on Social Security." Dale Carnegie was ahead of his time. This is a book of lists, and this section is "Six Ways to Make People Like You."

- Become genuinely interested in other people.
- Smile.
- Remember . . . a man's name.
- Be a good listener. Encourage others to talk about themselves.
- Talk in the terms of the other man's interest.
- Make the other person feel important and do it sincerely.

The third section is "Twelve Ways to Win People to Your Way of Thinking," and the final section is "Nine Ways to Change People Without Giving Offense or Arousing Resentment." The last of these principles is "Make the other person happy about doing what you suggest." Although it is in vogue to poke fun at Dale Carnegie in leadership circles, his book could be considered a bible for the leadership industry. His techniques and tactics parallel the principles that are so often promoted by leadership gurus.

Presidential Personalities

Personality has far more to do with leadership than one might imagine. In their groundbreaking book *Personality, Character, and Leadership in the White House*, professors of psychology Steven Rubenzer and Thomas Faschingbauer assess personality factors that presidents held in common and how these factors related to their leadership capabilities and overall effectiveness. Their questionnaires, based on "three major instruments designed to assess the full scope of personality," including IQ measuring devices, was sent to more than one hundred historians, biographers, and other specialists. The fundamental question was, "Does a president's personality predict his performance as president?" The study entailed three major goals related to leadership:

1. to objectively assess the personality of each president and render detailed personality portraits of those of greatest interest;
2. to identify the traits and personal qualities of successful and unsuccessful presidents;
3. to create a typology of presidents based on their personalities.

The authors also compared "the personalities of modern Democratic and Republican presidents" and examined "how the personality of our presidents has changed over time."[7]

There are many methods by which one can rate personalities—some that often seem somewhat contrived. But the methodology (the "Big Five" Personality Traits) used by these authors appears to be more sophisticated.

Psychoanalysis focuses on unconscious conflicts. The Myers-Briggs Type Indicator, a popular test used in business and counseling centers, measures a person's preference in directing his or her attention and processing information. The trait approach we use is based on a fifty-plus year program of research on people in real-life settings. Though based on completely familiar terms, like "friendly" and "generous," it is grounded in science. Unlike many other approaches, the "Big Five" model of personality is not based on theory, but on research on how people actually describe themselves.[8]

The "Big Five"

The "Big Five" scale that the authors utilize is one that is useful for all those contemplating their own personality traits and how those traits relate to their interpersonal relationships, whether at home or in the workplace. Interestingly, the traits do not predict whether one will be a leader—or even an effective leader. The presidents were all over the map on these traits. The "Big Five" are:

- Neuroticism (versus Emotional Stability): High scorers are moody, tense, self-conscious, prone to feeling downhearted and discouraged, and have difficulty resisting their impulses. High scorers among presidents include Nixon . . . and Lyndon Baines Johnson.

- Extraversion: Those scoring high in Extraversion are sociable, enthusiastic, energetic, adventurous, talkative, assertive, and outspoken. . . . Theodore Roosevelt (TR), Clinton, and Harding all scored very high.

- Openness to Experience: This dimension contrasts poets, philosophers, and artists with farmers, machinists, and "down-to-earth" people who have little interest in theories, aesthetics, or fanciful possibilities. High scorers like Jefferson and Lincoln are original, creative, and idealistic.

- Agreeableness: High scorers are sympathetic, kind, forgiving, appreciative, trusting, softhearted, modest, and considerate. . . . Few presidents score high on this scale, but Lincoln and Harding topped the list.

- Conscientiousness: High scorers like Wilson, Washington, and Carter are organized, thorough, hardworking, principled, deliberate, precise, and dependable.[9]

Character

In addition to the "Big Five," the authors added scales to measure "character," with items in their questionnaire relating to matters such as "lies, cheats, and steals" or "had many sexual affairs" as well as whether or not the president was "of good moral character." As it turned out—and perhaps not surprisingly—the "average president scores a bit below most Americans on Character

(42nd percentile)." Yet, a low score on aspects of Character ("low Straightforwardness"), at least for modern presidents, was often paired with "high Achievement." Apparently these modern *leaders* achieve more when they are more deceptive—as is often true among *leaders* in business and industry and, could we say, the church. What was perhaps most surprising from this study was that presidents "are barely more Competent (capable, showing sound judgment) than the average person."[10] What does that say about *leadership*?

"Low scores on character include Lyndon Johnson, Nixon, Jackson, John Adams, and Clinton"—Johnson's being the lowest, though "Clinton's ratings were obtained in 1995, before the scandal that resulted in his impeachment trial." The researchers discovered that character, however, "has *no* relationship to Presidential Success."[11]

Determining the standard of success was based on a variety of factors that have been used in both the private and public sector for many years, and here again the authors offer analysis that might seem obvious to presidential historians and observers: "Our research leads us to conclude that the most successful presidents have been ambitious, intelligent, assertive, and competent—but not necessarily straightforward or brimming with integrity."[12]

In this study, the authors point out some very significant aspects of leadership that have changed over time. "Modern presidents," the scales showed, "score higher on Need for Power: They want to have impact and prestige, to be in charge, and they want people to know it." The authors are not saying, however, that the need for power is necessarily a negative quality for leadership: "Though we fear power-hungry people, power motivation is associated with better performance in the White House."[13]

This study of presidents has profound implications for the study of leadership today in secular society as well as in the church. It is easy to insist that integrity, for example, must go hand-in-hand with leadership, but in reality the very factors that lead to "success" often fly in the face of integrity. President

Carter scores high on integrity but not on success—and so it is in business and very often in the church.

What is it then that makes a good leader? What makes a good president? Does a high score have far more to do with personality and charisma than with training? Top on the list of American presidents is Abraham Lincoln. He was a self-educated man who put far more stock in common sense than in a slick program on leadership.

Dale Carnegie's Lincoln

Lincoln the Unknown by Dale Carnegie is a surprisingly well-written biography. Originally published in 1932, its two hundred fifty pages can be read in a few evenings. It captures the personality of this man by someone who understood very well the power of personality—and particularly the power of winning friends and influencing people.

For those who dismiss the "Great Man" theory of leadership, Lincoln is an ever-present reminder that this old, washed-out theory stands the test of time. Of course it would be easy to argue that Lincoln demonstrates transactional leadership as seen in the effective transactions between him and those he worked with. But such theory does not explain the place Lincoln holds in history. Lincoln's personality—his intellect, his integrity, his common sense, his humor and story-telling capacity, his perseverance—served him well during his lifetime and in the generations since his death. Even his death served him well. As a martyr and hero, his place in history was established for all posterity.

Carnegie quotes a familiar section from the Lincoln biography written by law partner William Herndon. Here we see the very core of his personality that carried him through his presidency:

> In the afternoon of his last day in Springfield he came down to our office to examine some papers and confer with me about certain legal matters. . . . After these things were all disposed of

he crossed to the opposite side of the room and threw himself down on the old office sofa. . . . He lay for some moments, his face towards the ceiling, without either of us speaking. Presently he inquired, "Billy, . . . how long have we been together?" "Over sixteen years," I answered. "We've never had a cross word during all that time, have we?" To which I returned a vehement, "No, indeed we have not." He then recalled some incidents of his early practice and took great pleasure in delineating the ludicrous features of many a lawsuit on the circuit. . . . I never saw him in a more cheerful mood. He gathered a bundle of books and papers he wished to take with him and started to go; but before leaving he made the strange request that the sign-board which swung on its rusty hinges at the foot of the stairway should remain. "Let it hang there undisturbed," he said, with a significant lowering of his voice. "Give our clients to understand that the election of a President makes no change in the firm of Lincoln and Herndon. If I live I'm coming back some time, and then we'll go right on practicing law as if nothing had ever happened." He lingered for a moment as if to take a last look at the old quarters, and then passed through the door into the narrow hallway.[14]

This is the Lincoln who stands the test of time and who serves as a role model for all who would seek to expand their legacy footprint. Compare this Lincoln with packaged and programmed Donald T. Phillips' *Lincoln on Leadership: Executive Strategies for Tough Times*. The book bills itself as "the first book to examine Abraham Lincoln's diverse leadership abilities and how they can be applied to today's complex world." Here Phillips is reducing Lincoln to a set of principles. Each chapter makes a challenge to the one who would be a leader. For example, Chapter 2 is "Build Strong Alliances" and Chapter 3 is "Persuade Rather Than Coerce." Rather than letting Lincoln stand as a model, Phillips almost turns him into a twelve-step program. Indeed, at the end of each chapter there is a list of several "Lincoln Principles." Here the one who wants to be a leader like Lincoln learns things such as "everyone likes a compliment" and "you must seek and require access to reliable and up-to-date information."[15]

Leaders like Lincoln demonstrate the power of personality. They are both born and made—made through hard knocks and difficult circumstances and deep friendships. Leaders are not made by following a list of principles. If it were that simple, we might have had a dozen Lincolns running for president in 2008. We had none.

9

GIRL SCOUTS AND MORE

Gender and Leadership Reconsidered

Women have for centuries been recognized as talented listeners, nurturers, motivators, excellent communicators. These very qualities that we once were told were unbusinesslike are precisely the qualities that business needs most to tap human potential.

—Mary Cunningham Agee

Men don't ask for directions. When they are lost—though they never admit they are lost—they do not risk their manliness with the ego-threatening act of asking for directions, so the theory goes. The jokes are effortless: *Why did Moses wander for forty years in the wilderness? Because he refused to stop and ask for directions.*

More than a dozen years ago, in the fall of 1995, I was facing off against John Piper (author and minister of Bethlehem Baptist Church in Minneapolis) in a debate held in the Wheaton

College auditorium that drew a large crowd—standing room only. It was a hot topic: "What the Bible Says about Gender Roles." Piper began by taking a strong stand in favor of male-only headship. My position was that leadership (or headship) is not gender specific. At one point in my presentation I chided my opponent, quoting his written words on this very matter of asking for directions:

> Dr. Piper offers a . . . picture of the true woman—or, in his words, "mature femininity." The illustration he uses is a man asking for directions—which in itself seems to be an oxymoron. As Deborah Tannen and others have humorously pointed out, most men would rather stay lost than ask for directions. But this is the example Dr. Piper uses:
>
>> A housewife in her backyard may be asked by a man how to get to the freeway. At that point she is giving a kind of leadership. She has a superior knowledge that the man needs and he submits himself to her guidance. But we all know that there is a way for that housewife to direct the man that neither of them feels their mature femininity or masculinity compromised. (*Recovering Biblical Manhood and Womanhood*, 50)
>
> Whether in the church or in society at large, there continues to be debate as to how men and women ought to behave differently, or how they in fact do behave differently. That a "housewife" giving directions should be construed as an example of leadership is dubious in itself, but that she should be deferential because of her gender is part of our cultural consciousness that has deprived women of leadership opportunities. Even if a biblical or traditional case could be made to deny women the priesthood or other ministerial offices, to counsel women to be submissive when she is simply giving directions is ludicrous.

My less-than-submissive response to Piper's directive was that the next time a man stops by to ask directions of a "housewife in her backyard" she should just *tell him where to go*.

Gender Differences

It is true that by her very nature a woman might give directions differently than a man would, and that she might lead a corporation differently than her male counterpart. Indeed, there is a significant gender gap in the practice and theory of leadership. Women, due to both nature and nurture, often function differently than do men. But that women should be instructed to be ever conscious of potentially threatening a man's masculinity, be it a stranger or co-worker, feeds a man's insecurities as well as her own.

Such insecurities serve to hold women back in leadership roles. As I type these words into my computer, I'm crowded into the middle of the row, seat 25B, on Northwest flight 365 to San Francisco. I look around me on this Tuesday morning and see what appears to be primarily business travelers, more men than women but probably a ratio of about two to one. But first class is an entirely different matter. Due to the full flight, we were slowed down while boarding. Standing motionless in first class, I counted heads. There were twenty-one men and only three women—a ratio of seven to one.

This airline algebra is obviously anecdotal (though I have often observed similar ratios). And numbers certainly don't tell the whole story. Perhaps all of the female CEOs were sitting back in the cattle-car section with me in their concern for the company bottom line. Maybe the twenty-one suits in first class were househusbands dressed up for their annual getaway. But I suspect the numbers reflect what we all know—that women, in large percentages, have a long way to go before breaking through the glass ceiling in business, government, and the church. In fact, American women in the political realm are way behind women in other countries. More than eighty countries—including Canada, Mexico, Cuba, Vietnam, and Rwanda—have a higher percentage of women legislators than does the United States.[1]

Do men naturally excel in the arena of leadership? Is testosterone a factor? Are boys more often than girls pushed into competitive situations? Has the literature of male headship succeeded? However one may respond to those questions, it is unfortunate when leadership is perceived as a king-of-the-hill endeavor. Is it entirely possible that women are better programmed than men for leadership—whether in the church or in the world?

Biblical Headship

The debate over headship among evangelicals is now decades old. Years ago I wrote (and published) a historical study on the Greek word *kephale*, meaning "head." The issue was whether the word in its original context and its historical usage meant ruler or leader (as in *head* of a country) or if it meant source or origin. The contemporary usage is typically the former, but in ancient times the word often referred to origin. The other key Greek word was *authentein*. It is a word used once by Paul (1 Timothy 2) for authority. The key question is: Are women not to *exercise*, or are they not to *usurp*, authority? It makes a difference how one interprets the word. I have argued elsewhere (with coauthor and Greek scholar Walter L. Liefeld) that if Paul meant the former he would have most likely used the ordinary word for authority, *exousia*. He did not. Rather, he used an obscure term that many scholars believe meant to grasp or usurp. Paul references elsewhere women who were illegitimately grasping authority. In 1 Timothy 2, he rebukes such conduct. Such rebukes were surely not aimed exclusively at women.

But what does it all matter? Two decades ago the debate over Paul and women was on the front burner of my concerns. No longer. I'm convinced that Paul probably spoke out of both sides of his mouth on the matter. We only have to read Romans 16 to know that he had many important co-workers who were women, among them Phoebe (a deacon), Priscilla (often named before her husband Aquila), and Junia (who many believe was listed among the apostles). But Paul was living in a culture where women were considered little more than slaves and other property. I might wish that he would have spoken up like a man and made an unambiguous appeal for women's full equality, but he did not.

Even if Paul was as *conservative* on the matter of women's roles as many people claim, he was also *conservative* on the matter of slavery and fashion and many other cultural norms that we no longer practice today. So the issue rests not so much on understanding the precise words of Paul but rather on how we interpret and apply those words today.

Nevertheless, the idea that only men should be leaders is deeply imbedded in religion and culture. Emil Brunner, a twentieth-century Swiss theologian, considered by some to be the chief proponent of neo-orthodoxy, sums up what for many has been the Christian perspective on men and women:

> The man is the one who produces, he is the leader; the woman is receptive, and she preserves life; it is the man's duty to shape the new; it is the woman's duty to unite it and adapt it to that which already exists. . . . The man must build, the woman adorns; the man must conquer, the woman must tend. . . . It is the duty of the man to plan and to master, of the woman to understand and to unite.[2]

On the matter of women's leadership, biblical interpretations and applications have steadily changed over the generations. Because of these convictions, women were for centuries denied standard human rights such as testifying in a court of law, owning property, voting, holding office, and various other civil liberties that today are taken for granted. Interestingly, evangelicals in the nineteenth century were in the forefront of women's rights (and anti-slavery) movements. In recent decades, however, when it comes to issues of race and gender, evangelicals typically bring up the rear—if that.

Femininity, Language, and Put-downs

For women who enjoy a significant measure of equal rights with men, the matter of femininity need not be troubling.

Female is feminine; male is masculine. But many men—ones who are thoroughly secure—will admit to having *feminine* traits. For women, to admit having masculine traits is easier. A girl who is a *tomboy* or a woman who is strong and assertive (if indeed such a trait is masculine), this admission can be positive, especially when contemplating leadership. In my early adult years, men who were preparing for careers in nursing, elementary teaching, or secretarial work were thought to be stepping down to *women's work*. Women who aspired to the male professions like law or engineering, on the other hand, were moving up the ladder.

I remember the earlier days of the modern feminist movement when we were conditioned to hear certain words as put-downs. I flinched when I heard women called *ladies*. And the hair stood up on the back of my neck when I heard someone talking about the *girls* in the office. Today I'm more relaxed about the term *ladies*, probably because *we've come a long way, baby*. But the *girl* thing still bothers me—unless it is used by feisty ladies who spell it girrrrl. In the late 1970s when I was teaching at Grand Rapids School of the Bible and Music, I picked up a copy of the newly printed, pocket-size basketball schedule. On the front side was Men's Basketball; on the back Girls' Basketball. I suddenly had a cause. I marched into the office of the athletic director and demanded to know what was going on. I would settle for nothing less than men and women or girls and boys—or maybe women and boys. He was taken aback, musing aloud that the girls should feel fortunate that they are included on the schedule at all. But I was tenacious. The current year's schedule, he argued, could not be changed, but he did promise that there would be gender equity in the wording from that point forward.

Do words really matter? some might ask. Yes, they do. When a "housewife" is instructed to be deferential to the male ego in giving directions, words matter. Words matter for all human interaction. Slaves were kept in their place in part through words. *Boy* was the term for a man who was a slave. Imagine the sting every time that word was sounded.

110

Ain't I a Woman?

The significance of words and gender comes alive in the powerful cadence of Sojourner Truth's "Ain't I a Woman?" speech given at the Women's Rights Convention in Seneca Falls, New York, in 1852. The following description captures the atmosphere:

> Sojourner walked to the podium and slowly took off her sunbonnet. Her six-foot frame towered over the audience. She began to speak in her deep, resonant voice: "Well, children, where there is so much racket, there must be something out of kilter, I think between the Negroes of the South and the women of the North— all talking about rights—the white men will be in a fix pretty soon. But what's all this talking about?"
>
> She pointed to one of the ministers. "That man over there says that women need to be helped into carriages, and lifted over ditches, and to have the best place everywhere. Nobody helps me any best place. *And ain't I a woman?*"
>
> She raised herself to her full height. "Look at me! Look at my arm." She bared her right arm and flexed her powerful muscles. "I have plowed, I have planted and I have gathered into barns. And no man could head me. *And ain't I a woman?*"
>
> "I could work as much, and eat as much as man—when I could get it—and bear the lash as well! *And ain't I a woman?* I have borne children and seen most of them sold into slavery, and when I cried out with a mother's grief, none but Jesus heard me. *And ain't I a woman?*" . . .
>
> "That little man in black there! He says women can't have as much rights as men. 'Cause Christ wasn't a woman." She stood with outstretched arms and eyes of fire. "Where did your Christ come from?"
>
> "*Where did your Christ come from?*" she thundered again. "From God and a woman! Man had nothing to do with him!"
>
> The entire church now roared with deafening applause.
>
> "If the first woman God ever made was strong enough to turn the world upside down all alone, these women together ought to be able to turn it back and get it right-side up again."[3]

Sojourner Truth, like most of her female feminist counterparts, judged herself alongside men and found herself fully equal on their terms. She, like other women (and African Americans), had to prove her equality before she could demonstrate that women actually have an advantage over men in some endeavors.

Management and Negotiation

In *The 7 Habits of Highly Effective People*, Stephen Covey argues that management is different from leadership: "Leadership is primarily a high-powered, right brain activity. It's more of an art."[4] Such brain activity is out of sync with the "left brain–dominant world" we live in that enthrones such things as logic and statistics and subordinates that which is artistic and creative and intuitive.[5] It is no secret that women on the average tend to score lower in logic and higher in intuition.

There are other differences as well. "Sociological studies indicate that women's management styles differ significantly from those of men," write Ruth Howes and Michael Stevenson. "Women are less hierarchical. They organize on a broader base and prefer structures that are less like pyramids. Women in groups are less prone to self-assertion and more prone to compromise."[6]

Women have a leadership advantage when negotiation is preferred over an authoritarian style. Studies have shown that women police officers are often better equipped psychologically and in communication skills than are their male counterparts. A woman more easily diffuses a tense situation than her male partner who may inadvertently escalate the situation by his more authoritarian approach. This difference relates to leadership roles across the board. Men more than women are more prone to one-upmanship. The male ego is more than a mere myth. It can easily derail otherwise competent leadership.

Male Dominance and Female Leadership

In *Why Men Rule: A Theory of Male Dominance*, Steven Goldberg argues in a nutshell that testosterone more than anything else explains male dominance. And the corresponding lower levels of testosterone in women explain their inclination to gravitate to nurturing roles. His work is at times complex and provocative and not easily summarized in a few sentences. The book, originally published under the title *The Inevitability of Patriarchy*, drew heavy criticism from feminists and others. But history substantiates his theory. Dominant men rule— whether in battle or bullfighting or bureaucratic government or business.

Such a claim certainly does not suggest that such rule is superior to that which would be more nurturing. In fact, it can easily be argued that the opposite is true. In a column entitled "Female bosses rate higher as effective leaders: What must employers and males do?" Jim Collison makes that very case. Here are some of his citations:

> The Hagberg Consulting Group study. This consulting group, in Foster City, CA, examined evaluations of 425 high-level executives. Each was evaluated by about 25 people. The women execs won higher ratings on 42 of the 52 skills measured.
>
> The Personnel Decisions International study. This consulting firm, in Minneapolis, MN, examined 58,000 managers. It gave women the advantage in 20 of 23 areas.
>
> The Lawrence A. Pfaff and Associates study. Pfaff, of Kalamazoo, MI, examined evaluations from 2,482 execs and found that women outperformed men on 17 of 20 measures.
>
> The Management Research Group study. Robert Kabacoff, vice-president at the Portland, ME, organization, conducted the study. He compared male and female managers at the same firms, with similar jobs, at the same management level, and with the same amount of supervisory experience. He examined 1,800 supervisors in 22 management skills. The women outranked the men on about half the measures.
>
> The Janet Irwin study. She's a California management consultant. Her study involved more than 6,400 questionnaires. Women ranked higher than men on 28 of 31 measures.
>
> The Copernicus study. The survey of marketing executives by this firm, in Westport, CT, reported that 73% of respondents said men make decisions without input from others . . . while only 20% said the same thing about women.

That's six studies, done in a variety of ways, among a variety of people, in various parts of the U.S. All, excepting the Management Research Group study, conclude that female bosses have an edge over male bosses. And that study ranks them even.[7]

Collison's thesis is not that women are better than men. Rather the focus is on their particular skills and characteristics—ones that apparently come more naturally to women. If we were living in a time and place that highly rated authoritarian leadership, then Goldberg's "theory of male dominance" would be applicable. But such dominance does not work well in the twenty-first century— if it ever worked well. And it certainly does not mesh with the servant style that has been the theme of many leadership books. One might well ask if women were the political leaders of this world, would not diplomacy trump troop deployment?

Kathy Cloninger, Girl Scout CEO

If that were the case, should not girls be trained for leadership positions? And that is precisely what Kathy Cloninger, the CEO of Girl Scouts, hopes to do. As a visionary leader herself, it is her mission to "revitalize a 95-year-old tradition-bound icon"—an icon that for many people means "camps, crafts and cookies." She was frustrated by the fact that for decades the word that followed Girl Scout was "cookies" so she asked, "If we weren't about cookies, what *were* we about?" It is her goal to transform the image of these clubs into "the nation's premier leadership-development organization for girls."[8]

This new focus for Girl Scouts does not diminish the accomplishments of this near century-old symbol of American goodness. Juliette Gordon Low founded the movement in 1912, and in the decades since, girls have been trained as leaders.

They tended children while their mothers voted for the first time in the 1920s, led relief efforts during the Depression, supported the civil-rights movements of the '60s and launched a national environmental program. Alumnae include Laura Bush, Hillary

114

Clinton, Katie Couric and Eileen Collins, the first woman space shuttle commander.
Cloninger . . . initiated the first global poverty summit.[9]

When she was asked to submit her name for the top job in the Girl Scouts, Cloninger was the hands-on leader of the Tennessee Girl Scout council. So hands-on that when she received the call on her cell phone she was not in her office but off with girls "in a tent in a Texas meadow of bluebonnets." But she was not without resources: "Computer-savvy campers helped retrieve my résumé from my home computer, update it and e-mail it" on to the Girl Scouts' headquarters.[10]

Gone are the days when leadership is equated with male dominance. Leadership is teamwork, communication, sharing information, and consulting rather than dictating. Perhaps this is simply part of good management.

From the time of Juliette Gordon Low in the early twentieth century to that of space shuttle commander Eileen Collins, opportunities for girls have literally skyrocketed. And Cloninger vows to propel the rocket of leadership even higher. All well and good. But true *leadership*—that which is modeled by Low, Collins, and Cloninger herself—is rare. Few there be that find it. The challenge for girls—and for boys—is to be ever conscious of legacy. Legacy-thinking opens vistas that leadership-thinking does not. For the girl who has no inclination of leading a corporation, there may be dreams of writing a book—dreams that may not take shape until much later in life.

So it was with J. K. Rowling, a single mother on welfare. Today, with seven *Harry Potter* books, movies, and much more, her influence is immense. "Starting with that first letter [to a publisher], she has orchestrated a sustained dramatic crescendo unlike anything literature has ever seen"—more than three hundred million books in sixty-six languages. But some, including Lev Grossman, would suggest her legacy has been a mixed bag:

> Rowling's work is so familiar that we've forgotten how radical it really is. Look at her literary forebears. In *The Lord of the Rings*, J. R. R. Tolkien forged his ardent Catholicism with a deep,

115

nostalgic love for the unspoiled English landscape. C. S. Lewis was a devout Anglican whose *Chronicles of Narnia* forms an extended argument for Christian faith. Now look at Rowling's books. What's missing? If you want to know who dies in *Harry Potter*, the answer is easy: God.[11]

Perhaps the next series of bestselling fantasy books will be written by a girl who brings God back into the wonderful world of imagination. And perhaps we will move beyond the wonderful world of imagination as girls grow up to be world leaders in the realm of reality.

10

WHERE HAVE ALL THE FOLLOWERS GONE?

Submission and Authority Reconsidered

An appropriate American folk tune for the twenty-first century draws its lyrics from Pete Seeger:

> Where have all the followers gone?
> Long time passing
> Where have all the followers gone?
> Long time ago
> Where have all the followers gone?
> Girls have dissed them every one
> When will they ever learn?
> When will they ever learn?
>
> Where have all the young girls gone?
> Long time passing
> Where have all the young girls gone?
> Long time ago

Where have all the young girls gone?
In-de-pen-dent every one
When will they ever learn?
When will they ever learn?

I leave it to the reader to rephrase the remaining verses. The point is, *where have all the followers gone?* They are disappearing in alarming numbers. Without followers, the leadership industry is doomed to extinction. We can only imagine the devastation of our great American institutions if the "leadership Dow Jones" were to drop precipitously and crash. It would mean a sudden end to the glitzy, glossy, pricey seminars and conferences. As with other key market sectors, such a downturn would have a ripple effect—airlines, technology, tourism, food/lodging, and related enterprises. Unlike the oil industry, the leadership industry cannot fall back on imports. Foreign followers are barred by increasingly restrictive immigration laws. Robotics is an alternative but is too impersonal for the softer style expected of leaders today. The option that carries the most promise is primates. They can be trained to submit and follow simple directions with proper deference. They could quickly revolutionize the industry. Introductory and advanced training workshops would facilitate the development of transactional leader/ primate interfacing and would spur research leading to new book titles and corresponding conferences and institutes.

On a more serious note, *where* are the followers? In order to supply the ever-increasing numbers of leaders, there must be an even greater production of followers. This is a critical—and overlooked—issue when dealing with the topic of leadership. Followers, by their very nature, are defined in relation to leaders. Peter Drucker, one of the most prominent names in the leadership industry, is straightforward and succinct: "The only definition of a leader is someone who has followers."[1] Malcolm Forbes agrees: "No one's a leader if there are no followers."[2] In reference to CEOs, Tom Atchison writes, "Without committed followers, you have nothing but a title."[3] According to Warren Bennis (author of more than twenty-five leadership books), there must be "a transaction between leaders and followers. Neither could exist without the other."[4]

John Maxwell, also well-known in the field of leadership—especially in Christian circles—offers a contrasting perspective, drawing significant distinctions between leaders and followers: (1) leaders initiate, while followers react; (2) leaders pick up the phone and make contact, while followers wait for the phone to ring; (3) leaders spend time planning and anticipate problems, while followers spend time living day to day reacting to problems; (4) leaders invest time with people, while followers spend time with people; (5) leaders fill the calendar by priorities, while followers fill the calendar by requests.[5] By his standard, the follower ought to be sitting on a stool in the corner donned in a dunce cap.

But there have been many efforts to redeem the role of the follower in recent years—in many ways similar to the efforts of evangelical "complementarians," who seek to redeem the traditional restrictive role for women. The argument is that women are fully equal to men before God even though they are denied opportunities for ministry that men enjoy. Women, they say, are fully equal, but they are to submit to male authority—in the church and in the home. So also is the status of followers. Like women, they are now elevated in much of the literature to the same, equal plane as that of leaders. It may sound like a nice promotion, but it is doublespeak—and dishonest. In reality, we all know the follower is on a lower level than the leader, a level that reflects a lower salary and fewer benefits and perks.

Followership

In an online article entitled "Courageous Followers, Courageous Leaders," Ira Chaleff of exe-coach.com writes about the "role of courageous followers." Pointing to the "endless attention" that is paid to leadership, he asks: "Who ever pays attention to how well these same individuals perform their role as courageous followers? Virtually no one. Why is this?" He answers his own question:

> We are a society in love with leadership and uncomfortable with followership, though the subjects are inseparable. We don't honor followership. We talk pejoratively of followers being weak individuals. And we certainly don't train staff how to be strong followers who are not only capable of brilliantly supporting their leaders, but can also effectively stand up to them when their actions or policies are detrimental and need rethinking.[6]

I did not know there was a term *followership* until I began researching this book. I entered the word on Google and got 215,000 results (in November of 2007). Indeed, the term had its own Wikipedia entry. However, I note with a sigh of relief that it shows up as a misspelling on my spell-check. My own take on the term is to drop it entirely. It is a pitiful attempt to placate the masses by well-placed individuals in the ivory towers of leadership.

The notion of followership as a noble calling was popularized by Robert Kelley (business professor and management consultant) in a 1988 *Harvard Business Review* essay "In Praise of Followers" as well as in his book *The Power of Followership*. His intention was to challenge the negative stereotype of followers and give credibility and status to the role. The dismissive view of followers was blamed on social Darwinism that touted the survival of the fittest. The fittest are the leaders and the unfit—the losers— are the followers. "The result," according to one source, "is a hierarchical social topography, as if only leaders matter while the remaining 90 to 99 percent of the world is inferior and not worth mapping."[7] Few would agree that followers are "not worth mapping," but their inferior status is a given. Efforts to equalize leaders and followers are patronizing. "Just as there can be no front of an object without a back," we learn from the *Encyclopedia of Leadership*, "there can be no leaders without followers and no followers without leaders. Each depends on the other for existence and meaning."[8]

But as with front over back, leader is preferred over follower. The backseats in the theater are the least desirable. Having one's display in the front of the store is better than the back. And being relegated to the back of the bus was not equality for African

Americans. Trying to flatter the follower may appear to be good psychology, but it is insulting. Followers know full well that when leader means CEO or manager and follower means working stiff, there is a huge divide in remuneration, social status, and lifestyle. While the so-called followers typically accept that chasm, they rightly resent phony attempts to pretend the divide doesn't exist.

Yet there is a lucrative future for the *followership* fad. The book titles tell the story: *The Courageous Follower* (2003), *Followership: A Practical Guide* (2004), *Dynamic Followership* (2005), *Beyond Leadership to Followership* (2006), *Rethinking Followership* (2006), *The Art of Followership* (2008), *Followership: How Followers Are Creating Change* (2008).

Cooking the Books

With the flood of leadership training programs, it is only natural to assume that the number of leaders has been steadily increasing. But has there been a corresponding increase in the number of followers? Leadership literature rarely analyzes the mathematics of this necessary requisite. Such a requisite almost turns the concept of leadership into a Ponzi scheme. Every newly trained leader must have followers, just as every Amway distributor must have distributors making sales on a rung below. As with the increase in Amway leader-distributors, there must be a multiplication of distributor followers. So also with leadership. As the number of leaders increases, the number of followers must necessarily grow exponentially.

But if there is in actuality no such Ponzi scheme in the field of leadership, how do the numbers add up? Where do the followers come from? One way is to cook the books and count employees as followers. That the president or CEO of an organization is not automatically a leader is a difficult concept for many people to understand. For the sake of argument, we assume the CEO is the leader. But can we assume that the CEO has followers? In industry, most employees are workers who collect a paycheck

121

and eagerly anticipate weekends, vacation, and retirement. They are hardly "following the leader."

It is erroneous to imagine that employers and employees should be equated with leaders and followers. Nor are ordinary citizens to be mistaken for followers of those who wield political power. "Why, after all," writes Garry Wills, "should one person do another person's will? The answer that used to be given is simple: the leader is a superior person, to whom inferiors should submit. But modern democracies are [not] sympathetic to this scheme."[9]

Today most leadership gurus insist that the leader discovers what the people want and then casts a vision. But is that true leadership, and if so, who are the *followers*? Those who are essentially telling the so-called leader what to do? In the words of Wills, we are stuck "between two unacceptable alternatives—the leader who dictates to others, or the one who truckles to them." The leadership literature tends to proffer one or the other of these two alternatives. In the first instance, the leader is a "great man"—a role model who is "*worthy* of being followed—more disciplined than others, more committed, better organized." The other alternative is the leader who is ingratiating. "This is the salesmanship or Dale Carnegie approach—how to win friends and influence people. It treats followers as customers who 'buy' the leader's views."[10]

At the end of the day, who is willing to be numbered among the followers? Despite the efforts to pay homage to followers, they indeed are scarce. Is there any situation that should tempt me to want to be a leader with my own followers? I'm a teacher and a writer. I want people to consider my words—my ideas—and to perhaps make them their own for the cause of a higher principle, not to simply follow me.

Indeed, there are very few instances in life that call for a leader with followers. One of the most basic is perhaps parents and children—though rarely is the term leadership brought to bear on that relationship. Children must follow and obey their parents. But even at a young age children are by nature challenging that *leadership*. And rightfully so if they are to mature and develop a sense of independence from their parents.

Another situation that calls for a leader with followers is that of a guide—for example, in mountain climbing. I can't climb Mount Everest alone; the guide is the leader and I am the follower. He essentially controls my life for a specified endeavor and duration of time.

My husband is a leader. He is the conductor of Jubal Brass, an eighteen-member West Michigan brass ensemble. During rehearsals and performances, eighteen musicians have willingly agreed to follow his leadership—his conducting.

The military is still another example that involves legitimate leaders and followers. A sergeant who leads his soldiers through dangerous desert sands or infested swamps to rout the enemy is a leader with followers.

Blaming Followers

Although much of the literature on followers either serves to assure them that they are as important and worthy as are leaders or to offer them principles on how to be good followers, there is also a perspective that places blame on followers for the incompetence of the leaders. This is seen in the writing of Warren Bennis, who was chair of the Leadership Institute, University of Southern California, Marshall School of Business, and a longtime leadership expert now riding the wave of followership.

Bennis insists that followers must challenge leaders. In an article entitled "Followership," he offers an illustration of President Reagan's then vice president, George Bush, who approached Nancy Reagan (as she relates in her memoir *My Turn*) with his very serious concerns about the White House chief of staff Donald Regan:

> "I wish you'd tell my husband," the First Lady said. "I can't be the only one who's saying this to him." According to Mrs. Reagan, Mr. Bush responded, "Nancy, that's not my role."
> "That's exactly your role," she snapped.
> Nancy Reagan was right. It is the good follower's obligation to share his or her best counsel with the person in charge. And

silence—not dissent—is the one answer that leaders should re-fuse to accept.[11]

That Bush was a "follower" of Reagan is an odd use of the term, but even if he was, is he the one to blame for not chal-lenging Reagan? Bennis reasons that Reagan "suffered far more at the hands of so-called friends who refused to tell him unat-tractive truths than from his ostensible enemies." But to imagine that Reagan, the leader, was suffering at the hands of Bush, the follower, is unfair. A good leader is one who invites counsel and criticism. But all too often "followers" feel intimidated, and they stand by in silence.

Followers, however, are surely not to be viewed as entirely blameless. They know right from wrong, and they bear an ethical responsibility to stand up to leaders in the face of wrongdoing. One might think that soldiers in the heat of battle or young adults swayed by a charismatic cult leader would be most susceptible to the malady of *bad followership*. But often those who are presumed most sophisticated easily truckle.

In his writings on administrative mobbing in academia, Ken-neth Westhues lays out a pattern of how colleagues are often in collusion with the administrators in unfairly ridding a scholarly institution of one of its own. Westhues, a professor of sociology at the University of Waterloo in Ontario, uncovers behaviors of leaders and followers one might not expect in higher education. *Mobbing* is the term, and it is easily recognized—especially when compared to abuse sometimes seen in parenting. In *The Envy of Excellence: Administrative Mobbing of High-Achieving Professors*, he offers a healthy response to a child together with an abusive response:

> Compare two responses parents can make to a child who has just been eliminated from a spelling bee or gymnastics competition. They can say, "This just wasn't your day, we're sorry you won't be going on to the advanced level, better luck next time." Or they can say (what most of us have overheard on some occasion, and winced), "You stupid little ——, what's wrong with you, you've brought shame on your school, get out of my sight." . . . In the

first instance, the child's person is acknowledged and affirmed even in the midst of inadequate performance. In the second instance, a mistake is enlarged to cover and smear the child's whole identity. Only the second instance illustrates the process that is the focus of the present book.[12]

Workplace mobbing often begins with administrators (acting like abusive parents) targeting a professor (or other employee). But the target's colleagues—the followers—are necessary for support. Why would they prop up such abuse? "Most academics are so concerned about their jobs, their grants, the respect of their peer groups, and their good standing with superiors," writes Brian Martin, "that they are very unlikely to take an unpopular public stand" of supporting the colleague being attacked. Thus by their silence or through "malicious gossip and whispering campaigns," they join in the mobbing in an effort to promote—if not save—their own careers.[13]

By their collusion these followers have willingly participated in the mobbing initiated by the leader.

Fooled Followers

Followers come in various stripes. Some are fooled by the leader; others follow with their eyes wide open, hoping to score points. A letter written to advice columnist Jeanne Marie Laskas sums up a typical situation:

> A few months ago, they hired a new guy at my level. He's a classic kiss-up—gets coffee for our two assistant managers, gives them little gifts. That's his main work ethic; productive he is not. But they've made him the third in charge. I'm not jealous, just fed up that he's bought himself special treatment. What recourse do I have?[14]

The response, in my mind, was ill-conceived. Laskas suggested the writer "try some humor. . . . Next time he comes in with lattes, hand him an all-day sucker in front of your superiors." My own experience tells me such a gesture would backfire. The writer needs to be looking around for a position where productivity is rewarded.

Identifying oneself as a follower means placing great trust in a leader and thus carrying with it corresponding responsibility for the leader's actions. Followers are sometimes rightly denigrated for being mindless and passive. They have the capacity to falsely elevate leaders in a way that turns a mediocre leader into a bad leader. I have seen it happen in various settings. The followers may be board members or parishioners or starry-eyed students, but they easily fall into a fan-club mentality. This is particularly true in religious settings. Whether seminary presidents or megachurch ministers, religious leaders (with worshipful admirers hanging on every word) easily become so narcissistic they imagine they can do no wrong. Their work and God's work become one and the same.

Eugene Peterson hits the nail on the head. He insists that the career ladder and the temptations associated with it are more sinister in the Christian world than in the corporate world— more sinister in the "world of religion, where I can manipulate people and acquire godlike attributes to myself. The moment I entertain the possibility of glory for myself, I want to blot out the face of the Lord and seek a place where I can develop my power." The lust for power is not unique to ministers and religious leaders, but they "have the temptation compounded because we have a constituency with which to act godlike. Unlike other temptations, this one easily escapes detection, passing itself off as a virtue."[15]

The *constituency* Peterson references is a synonym for *followers*, and the godlike power of leaders is equated with virtue. This is a most dangerous mix—leaders and followers—that easily explodes when the spark (or flame) of religion is added.

Werner's Followers

One of the most brazen examples of this was brought to mind as I was doing an online search for information on Professor

Warren Bennis, a leading voice in the field of leadership. I was surprised when I learned that he is pictured first on a website titled "Friends of Werner Erhard." I had somehow imagined that Erhard was sufficiently dead and buried (figuratively, if not literally) and that references to him would relate to the distant past of the 1970s. I did some further digging only to learn that Erhard was an invited guest for a celebration honoring Bennis in 2004 at Harvard University. With that, the search was on. How could it be that Bennis was ever a follower of Erhard? Well, we've all done foolish things in our younger years. But how, I still wonder, could he possibly be defending this man today? Is this an example of the inexplicable hold of leaders on followers that often continues despite all evidence to the contrary—evidence that the leader is bad, if not an utter fraud? If so, here then lies one more example of the danger of the leader-follower mix.

My knowledge of Werner Erhard dates back to the late 1970s when I began teaching courses on cults and new religions. A decade later my text *Another Gospel: Alternative Religions and the New Age Movement* was published. Although Erhard did not merit a chapter, his movement est (and later known as The Forum) is featured in appendix A, which offers shorter summaries of more than twenty lesser-known cultic groups. Erhard founded est in 1971, after he had abandoned his wife and four children and his job (as a used car salesman) and moved to California. There he assumed a new identity, leaving behind his old name—Jack Rosenberg—as well.

The 1970s and following was an era of new religions and quasi-religious groups that promoted a variety of self-help concepts. Est boasted followers who reported that "they have rid them-selves of medical problems, can lose weight without trying, are getting better jobs and forming better relationships, and feeling better about money, sex and God." Celebrities—including John Denver, Joanne Woodward, Cloris Leachman, Valerie Harper, Diana Ross, Jerry Rubin, and Yoko Ono—offered endorsements after participating in seminars billed as "60 hours that transform your life."[16]

Although praised by some, these seminars serve as a warning to those who herald the concept of followership. True, est illustrates an extreme form of intimidation, but even less abusive programs easily diminish the individual who is deemed a follower.

> An est seminar is a calculated process of breaking down the inductee's personality and then rebuilding it by harassment and intimidation. A trainer begins immediately to abuse the audience verbally with repeated obscenities. All ego defenses are ridiculed by means of demeaning epithets hurled at anyone who resists the tactics of the trainer. Eyewitnesses report that scores of people urinate, defecate, convulse, sob, scream, and vomit (in specially provided silver-colored est bags). Their only relief comes in the form of "meditation practices" . . . and exercises of lying on the floor to "find one's space."[17]

The climax of the seminar is the moment of enlightenment—when the trainee can testify that she becomes exactly what she wanted to be. That such a training program could actually result in personal growth is difficult to imagine. Indeed, testimonials that show the exact opposite are numerous—and most specifically in Erhard's own family. A CBS 60 Minutes documentary conducted by Ed Bradley, well-known for his fair-minded investigative journalism, portrayed Erhard as a man who was consumed with controlling his *followers*, whether family or cult devotees. Children (from two marriages) testified to his terrorizing them—and not just with verbal threats. Beatings and rape and incest were all part of his abusive tactics. Co-workers testified to taking part in the cruelty both to curry favor and to avoid being targeted themselves. Erhard denied the accusations, and "Friends of Werner Erhard" insist that the stories are exaggerated.

But having watched the 60 Minutes taped program with my husband and stepdaughter on the Thanksgiving weekend of 2007, we all agreed that such testimonies could not be faked. Their efforts to stifle their sobs and their anguished descriptions were far beyond the realm of good acting. And of the half dozen interviewed, their stories were eerily similar—with different perspectives and details—but all portraying an evil leader controlling his followers. The full story of Erhard's leadership is told in Steven Pressman's well-researched volume *Outrageous Betrayal: The Dark Journey of Werner Erhard from est to Exile* (New York: St. Martin's Press, 1993).

Werner's Friends

The Werner Erhards of this world should not shock us. But that a well-respected expert in the field of leadership, Warren Bennis, would defend the man and methods ought to alert us to the potentially "cultic" nature of the leadership industry. In an article entitled "The Return of Werner Erhard" in the *Los Angeles Magazine* (1988), Bennis stood by Erhard:

> Another scholar who knows Erhard well is Warren Bennis, professor of business administration at USC. Bennis took the est training in 1979 in London: "It gave me a good sense of who I was at a critical period in my life. I had just ended my time as university president, and I was looking around for new directions."
>
> Bennis, who during the early 1980s served as a consultant to Erhard, giving advice on organizational design and leadership techniques, felt that what the training provided in those years was a "restoration of the self." . . . "I have to say," adds Bennis, "that it's an incredible puzzle for me that he has acquired such a negative image among so many people. I detect a lot of hostility, and I don't understand it."[18]

Few individuals acquire "such a negative image among so many people" and draw such "a lot of hostility" without cause. For Erhard, the facts speak for themselves. For loyal followers, like Bennis, "incredible puzzle" is the best explanation. So it was that "in honor of his longtime friend, Warren Bennis," Erhard was among the household names of the leadership industry who attended the celebrative daylong gathering at Harvard University in 2004. Other guests included Jack Welch, Stephen Covey, Ken Blanchard, Ron Heifetz, Barbara Kellerman, Tom Peters, and James O'Toole.

That Bennis included his longtime friend on the guest list was his prerogative, and we must be careful of assigning guilt by association. But if the guest list included a Mafia boss or an exiled South American dictator instead of Erhard, even Harvard might have raised its eyebrows. For family members and followers damaged by est, Erhard is such a dictator boss whose leadership illustrates the potential dangers of *following*. Followers of Erhard in many instances fell under the terrorizing grip of power no less than did followers of Jim Jones and Hitler.

Bennis conceded that he had concerns, but he blamed the followers: "Another problem has been the dependence upon Werner himself. Which is not his problem. If you're in that kind of position, sometimes you get disciples as opposed to students"[19]—or, more precisely, *followers* as opposed to students.

By the very nature of the game, we too easily follow the leader—often to our own peril.

11

PRESIDENT OF THE INTERNET

Life without Leaders Reconsidered

Recently I googled a topic and the first site that showed up on my screen turned out to be a porn-peddling market-place—a site unrelated to the subject I was researching. I mentioned this to a friend who is a self-described computer illiterate. His response: "Why don't you just email the Internet and threaten to report them?" When I tried to explain that the Internet is an entity that has no central location that could be contacted, he picked on my original comment and said, "Well then, email Google." Sure. There simply is no president or—with all due respect to Al Gore—inventor of the Internet. There is no central command. There is no leader. The Internet is a chaotic, messy, democratic, libertarian—and very efficient—entity.

With all its faults and failures, the Internet is an incredible aid to research—and for this book in particular—although it will never replace the good old-fashioned library. But in some ways it trumps the stacks filled with books—or all too often stacks missing the very book I'm looking for. While at my computer, I can usually discover from reviews whether or not I need the actual book and then go to a library site and have the book reserved and perhaps sent to the little library near my home. Or I can find the book online and do keyword searches as I peruse it. But the Internet offers much more than books for the researcher.

The democracy of the Internet allows anyone to be an "expert." That is essentially true in the print media—whether books, magazines, newspapers, or advertising flyers. Indeed, in an era of self-publishing, anyone can be an author—and an expert. How then do we know what is true and what is not? One must be as discerning in this era of increasing *leaderlessness*—even as one should be in an era of authoritarian top-down decrees. Here is a perspective from an Internet "expert" on this trend away from leadership. The site is *Lead Well*.

> We are moving away from the traditional relationships involving a boss who told people what to do and subordinates who almost blindly followed the directives of their superiors. The emerging model is considerably more collaborative. Workers at all levels concentrate more on cooperating with each other than on giving orders for others to do things. The hierarchy in the work organization, honored since Max Weber introduced bureaucracy, is dissolving and will all but disappear within ten years. The lines of authority will blur as people work in self-developed teams, almost oblivious to management structures.[1]

Democracy and Leaderlessness

By its very nature, a democracy encourages a society operated largely without leaders. A totalitarian regime is precisely the opposite. Every group meeting and every individual act that appears out of the ordinary was watched and reported by a cog in the chain of command in the old Communist states of Russia and China—and perhaps even today to a lesser extent. The powerful leaders maintained control by developing a hierarchy of leadership that extended from the top down.

The situation is very different in a democratic state that fosters what is termed *rugged individualism*, supported by rights and freedoms. We cherish the First Amendment of the Bill of Rights: "Congress shall make no law respecting an establishment of religion, or prohibiting the free exercise thereof; or abridging the freedom of speech, or of the press; or the right of the people peaceably to assemble, and to petition the Government for a redress of grievances." I not only have the "freedom of religion" but also the freedom to disavow religion and the freedom to disavow the very Constitution that gives me these freedoms. Such *freedom* undercuts the very concept of leadership.

In an earlier era, prior to secular democracies—and more importantly the communications revolution—leadership was an aspect of life that was simply assumed. If the tribe or clan or prefecture or realm was ruled by a good leader, all the better. The leader led and the people followed. But today is leadership nearly obsolete? In most situations, I'm not well served by a visionary leader; for example, someone involved with my financial investments. Rather, I simply want good management. In presidential politics, a manager—even a do-nothing manager—will leave a far better legacy than a leader (and commander in chief) who presides over a costly military disaster and failed foreign policy that can never be undone. In church we see more leadership debacles than we see leadership triumphs.

Before the era of democracy and instant communications, leaders were deemed necessary and bad leadership was more easily mistaken as good. Christians looked to the pope and the lesser clerics as leaders that must be followed. But today we prize our independence. For good or for ill, we freely change churches and political allegiance without imagining we must follow a leader. Indeed, our need for leaders is primarily a need foisted on us by the leadership industry and those who aspire to that role.

Christ in Brussels

Has leadership become obsolete? Have leaders and followers become almost indistinguishable? Barbara Kellerman broaches that question with a critique of a work of art by Belgian artist James Ensor that I found fascinating. She draws from the observations of James O'Toole:

> *Christ's Entry into Brussels* is a vast canvas of particular people— including one leader and many followers—in a particular place. But the crowded and chaotic street scene leaves us uncertain. So O'Toole asks, "Where is Christ in all this confusion? Shouldn't he be in the forefront, *leading* the parade? Shouldn't he be the visual focus of the painting? . . . For nearly two millennia Christ—the leader/Redeemer—*was* the center of attention. But on this particular canvas, he is in the background, "almost lost in a throng of revelers that threatens to engulf him." O'Toole's point is that Ensor was the first to illustrate the modern condition: one in which secular democracy has rendered traditional forms of leadership nearly obsolete.[2]

This painting has profound implications for Christians. Those who say they are following Christ need to look at the canvas again. They are in the crowd, but they're going every which way in their party costumes. None on canvas or in real life appear to be bearing a cross and giving all they have to follow the leader. The Christian church has an abundance of would-be leaders but few who are willing to enter into Brussels following Christ.

The message of the painting also has implications that go far beyond the Christian community. The Western world that once followed Christ is milling around in the painting—Christians and non-Christians indistinguishable. And much of the world at large going every which way—leaderless.

The *Science* of Leadership and Leaderlessness

In this modern world (where postmodernism continues to pester with the tenaciousness of a yipping terrier), science continues to reign supreme. If one makes a case for a six-literal-day creation, science is utilized and sometimes seems to trump Scripture itself. It comes as no surprise then that science is brought to the table when leadership is under the microscope. Indeed, the science of leadership is at least a century old—a science "discovered" by Frederick Winslow Taylor. Taylor identified his new discipline as "scientific management" in part because it sought to break management down to its very essence by studying it in small parts—by investigating various basic tasks to understand how they could be accomplished most efficiently. Taylorism was a fad that has long since passed, but today's management consulting firms such as McKinsey continue to grant their specialty an air of scientific credibility. Do they succeed? "At their best, consultants see a situation with fresh eyes and bring some useful analytical tools," writes Michael Kinsley. "At their worst, they are a prestige play verging on a protection racket. Hey, Mr. CEO: Every other big company has hired McKinsey. What's your problem?"[3]

The *modern* science of management and leadership now has its competition in the more *postmodern* science of leaderlessness—a *science* that leaders in every field would do well to study. The book to read is *Leadership and the New Science: Discovering Order in a Chaotic World* by Margaret J. Wheatley. This volume is worlds away from Taylorism. Its science relates to the fields of quantum physics, self-organizing systems, and chaos theory. Wheatley does not advocate leaderlessness and chaos and anarchy as a hopeful wave of the future; rather, she offers balance. She looks to the natural world for a pattern. "This was a world where order and change, autonomy and control were not the great opposites that we had thought them to be. It was a world where change and constant creation were ways of sustaining order and capacity."[4]

In many ways, Wheatley is affirming a way of thinking and a style of doing things that I already find appealing. I embrace the chaos that I live in every day—especially the chaos in my mind. The questions far exceed the answers. I keep lists and notes not because of a need for orderliness but rather to keep track of the clashing ideas that are constantly bombarding me. My ease with multitasking surely has the appearance of chaos. But my life is not all chaos. The chaos is balanced by order. If not, a volume such as the one I am now writing might never be finished, certainly not by my contract deadline.

But the chaos that exists all around us is typically ignored or suppressed (as much as chaos can be suppressed). This is most counterproductive. Indeed, any *science* of management that fails to account for—and embrace—the chaos of the natural world and the chaos of organizations and the chaos of a thinking mind is substandard. "Each of us lives and works in organizations designed from Newtonian images of the universe," writes Wheatley. "We manage by separating things into parts, we believe that influence occurs as a direct result of force exerted from one person to another, we engage in complex planning for a world that we keep expecting to be predictable, and search continually for better methods of objectively measuring and perceiving the world." But this, she goes on to say, is in many ways outmoded science. "We need to stop seeking after the universe of the seventeenth century and begin to explore what has become known to us during the twentieth century. We need to expand our search for the principles of organization to include what is presently known about how the universe organizes."[5]

This world is one that "seeks order" and "knows how to organize itself without command, control, or charisma." In both the natural world and in the world of human relationships we observe self-organization. Wheatley illustrates this point with a section subtitled "Leadership in Disasters: Learning from Katrina." One sentence stands out: "Following any disaster, we see the best of human nature and the worst of bureaucracy" (though unfortunately, we also sometimes see the worst of human nature in the act of looting). Not only did FEMA itself seriously botch relief efforts, but it, as so often is the case, stymied volunteer work: "These self-organized efforts are often hindered by officials who refuse their offers, cite regulations, or insist that protocols and procedures be followed." In such disasters, "leaders are afraid to actually lead." That says it all. But at the end of the day, these so-called leaders have great power to make a bloody mess of things. The best leaders are most often individuals who (with no help from PowerPoint presentations) rise up and take charge when a situation calls for leadership. Who are the worst? "Senior leaders [who] find it difficult to act . . . spontaneously or independently.

136

Any independent response is constrained by the need to maintain the power and policies of the organization."[6]

Swarm Theory

What would happen in the world—or in America—if there were no leaders? America is a nation of laws and standards and regulations and systems. There are bureaucrats and managers and ordinary citizens of all varieties who keep society running smoothly often without a recognizable leader. In fact, the nation might function more effectively *without* a leader. Such is a credible conclusion drawn from swarm theory—a theory that has developed largely by studying insects and larger members of the animal kingdom. Ant colonies, beehives, flocks of birds, schools of fish, and herds of caribou all offer researchers valuable data on collective intelligence. In swarms they work efficiently without a leader.

This collective intelligence has implications for human efficiency as well. Trucking companies, for example, save mileage and money by allowing computer programs (drawn from the swarm theory of bees) to assign daily routes. Airlines are also utilizing swarm theory in developing air-traffic patterns.

I've personally seen human swarm theory in action. Some years ago when living in Indiana, weather reports told of serious flooding in a nearby town. When we arrived to help in the sandbagging, hundreds of volunteers were already there. Local (and distant) truckers and construction companies, through no organized effort, had delivered sand and sandbags. People swarmed in from miles around. No one appeared to be in charge. We simply joined the line and did what others were doing and helped save homes from the raging waters of the rising river. Such swarming in many situations is more efficient than calling in experts from far away.

"I used to think ants knew what they were doing," writes Peter Miller in a *National Geographic* article on swarm theory. "Turns out I was wrong." So how do ants carry out the seemingly complicated and ever-changing assignments needed to run an efficient anthill? It depends not on individual ants but on the colony.

> That's how swarm intelligence works: simple creatures following simple rules, each one acting on local information. No ant sees the big picture. No ant tells any other ant what to do. Some ant species may go about this with more sophistication than others. . . . But the bottom line . . . is that no leadership is required.[7]

Is it possible that we have been emphasizing the importance of leadership when what our society actually needs is more efficient swarming? Swarming relates to a localized community's instinctual collective concern for its own well-being, rather than having one individual—a so-called leader—cast a vision and inspire people to follow. Efficient swarming is always better than bad leadership and sometimes better than good leadership. The most foundational leadership question we must ask in any given situation is: Is leadership necessary?

The Starfish and the Spider

In researching what was turning out to be an "anti-leadership" book, I was for a while thinking that I had come up with a new concept. Everyone else is out there running around like a chicken with its head cut off, insisting that there must be a head of any effective organization—or organism. Then, along comes a book (published while I was doing the research) entitled *The Starfish and the Spider* arguing that the starfish does just fine without a head. A spider does not. In his review of that book, Robert D. Steele writes:

> I listened to Al Gore last night on Global Warming, in Boise, Idaho—10,000 people who gave him multiple standing ovations, and I plan to listen to George Bush on Iraq tonight. Al gets it, George does not. Centralized systems cannot defeat decentralized systems. Al Gore is leading a massive global campaign to get all of us to change the planet from the bottom up, while George

(or Dick Cheney, depending on who you think actually runs the place) is deepening America's loss of global standing and moral stature at the same time that he is bankrupting the treasury and destroying the Armed Forces—and planning a conventional attack on Iran at the same time. One of these guys is sane, the other is a nutcase. The good news is that decentralized morality can triumph over centralized corruption, and that is the back story on Al Gore's emergence as a virtual Earth Leader.[8]

Back to the book itself: *The Starfish and the Spider: The Unstoppable Power of Leaderless Organizations.* The authors are Ori Brafman and Rod A. Beckstrom, both Stanford MBAs. They argue that power and effectiveness and success are assumed to be associated with hierarchy—with organizations with a leader, be it a CEO or a five-star general or a university president. But in reality, there is incredible power in decentralization, and it is often far more effective. Whether assessing the power of the Internet (and such entities as Wikipedia) or Alcoholics Anonymous or Muslim terrorism, there is remarkable success in "organizations" (or *disorganizations*) that have no leader.

Such decentralization has occurred in religion. The Roman Catholic Church—though still under the authority of the Vatican—becomes more and more decentralized with each passing day as ordinary Catholics go their own way and find their own spirituality. For good or for ill, many have become very independent, paying little attention to decrees from on high. Such decentralization has occurred even more rapidly in Protestantism that began its process of decentralization in the sixteenth century. Today many top-down Protestant denominations are losing members while independent churches grow. The same has been true of cults and alternative religions. Christian Science, for example, a one-time powerful religious movement, is today but a skeleton of what it once was. Some of its most basic beliefs are now found in what is known as New Age. New Age is as loose and decentralized as a religion can get, and it is sometimes imagined to be on the wane because there are no powerful leaders lurking behind the mansion doors of a cult compound. But New Age is stronger than ever as a decentralized religion—whether it is perceived as postmodern religion or your garden-variety flim-flam mindless spirituality. New Age literature is no longer categorized as *New Age* in many bookstores, because its underlying worldview has seeped into so much of contemporary North American life.

The next form of religious decentralization will come as the megachurch phenomenon begins to weaken and die. The senior-pastor, top-down leadership style will lose its luster, and decentralization will occur in smaller community groups—ones identified with a neighborhood more than a denomination or personality.

"Where have all the leaders gone?" asks David Gergen. "As Americans survey a landscape that seems uncommonly bleak, a new national survey commissioned for . . . *U.S. News* found that two thirds of the public believes the nation is in a leadership crisis, while nearly three quarters worries that unless we find better leaders soon, the nation will begin to decline."[9] A lamentation for lost leaders, it would seem, might be in order. But it is not. America has leaders—bad leaders. But are "better" leaders (found soon) the solution to the problem? Or is a new understanding of leadership and leaderlessness a key to solving the problem? Does swarm theory or the starfish or new science have anything to say to Americans today—before it is too late?

PART II

CREATING A LEGACY

12

LEGACY 620

Bequeathing a Personal Legacy

If I were teaching Legacy 620 (instead of the Leadership 620 course I have previously taught), I would begin, as I usually do, with personal introductions that relate to the subject matter. I would ask students to briefly introduce themselves in relation to a legacy they have received or one they're in the process of passing along—or both. We would then discuss definitions and descriptions, knowing full well that a dictionary is not enough. Our stories bring to life this otherwise lazy noun. I would then assign a legacy essay. The students would begin with a stream-of-consciousness exercise—taking notes on their random thoughts. I can see them now with their laptop computers entering words as fast as they can type them in. The end product—perhaps not due until the end of the term—would bring flesh to the spiny skeleton but not with a look of completion.

This chapter is in part that sort of essay. My own random thoughts and stories are mixed in with those of others. The skeleton has flesh, but not to be mistaken for a completed form. And perhaps that's how we should contemplate legacy.

The Child Beside Me

The story of Jane Addams, founder of Hull House, is a fascinating case study of how one's inherited legacy influences a life. The "settlement" work among the poor of Chicago was a world away from the small-town life of her childhood. Yet she found it imperative to go back in her imagination in order to move forward. "Her own childhood," writes biographer Jean Bethke Elshtain, "provided the template on which she strove to understand sympathetically the very different childhoods of the teeming throng of young people in the 19th ward of Chicago, and by extension, the entire city and the world beyond." The backdrop for developing this template was a tour of Egypt when she was in her early fifties. It was here that "she sensed a tensile strand of memory and experience stretching across a vast distance— from the pyramids of Giza to the village cemetery in Cedarville, Illinois—and threading together past and present time."[1]

Halfway around the world and well into middle age, Addams began drawing on her childhood for inspiration. Then and there she realized she was accompanied "by a small person with whom I was no longer intimate." That lack of intimacy separated her from the little ones she most wanted to help. Calling forth memories of her childhood, she sought to understand fears and longings from a child's point of view. She recalled her own deepest fear—a death scene at the schoolhouse cemetery—and wrote it down. This became a tool for more effective ministry to both children and adults.

As I am reading this biography, I am challenged to contemplate my own childhood—and the child that walks alongside me. I have good memories of those years on a farm in northern Wisconsin, where I lived with my mother and father and four siblings. I was the middle child, a brother and sister older, and a brother and sister younger. Although I think and talk about this life so long ago and have used illustrations of my childhood in other writings, I have never actually sought to intimately know this child beside me. Only now am I seeking to understand the fears and aspirations of the little girl, the teenager, the young woman who has become my present self. This I do in order to more effectively serve others as did Jane Addams.

My Mother's Legacy

I think often of my mother who was killed in an auto accident at age fifty-seven—a story included in other of my writings. What a profound influence she had on me, far more than that of my aloof father who lived to the age of eighty-nine.

It's easy for me to reflect on only the good in my mother. But I can also imagine that neighbors in our farming community snickered to themselves that she was the one who wore the pants in the family. In fact, a childhood friend suggested as much a few years ago. My mother was an outspoken woman with a strong personality. It was she who reported Mr. Emerson—the teacher at the one-room Gaslyn Creek school—for beating my brother for sneaking away with a fishing pole on a warm spring afternoon. My father never would have done that. She was the one who drove from one farmhouse to the next, amid vocal opposition, collecting signatures to consolidate the country school with the larger city school system. Right or wrong, she was determined to fight for the best education possible for her five children. In the end, her petition drive succeeded.

Her legacy registers both positive and negative—not the least of which was her quick temper. Indeed, her fury had no measure when she spotted me across the gym sneaking out of a hometown basketball game with my boyfriend. Although her love had a fierceness and I never for a moment doubted it, there were many occasions when I wished she might have kept her distance. Some of my mother's flaws have been passed on—or picked up—and I see them when I look in the mirror. And the same process continues with my son. He is quick to praise me as a mother, but I must be ever aware of that mixed bag of genes that I have bequeathed to him.

Fortunately, we need not allow the negative inheritance to rule our lives. From his father, my son's inherited legacy has been mostly negative. An absent father surely does not mean absent legacy. For more than half of his life (nearly twenty years) he has not seen his father—or even had an address or phone number. There is no way to measure the harmful effects of abandonment, but he is determined that the same legacy will never be passed along in his relationship to his daughter. The Bible tells us that the sins of the fathers (and mothers) are passed along to the children. How true. And how important it is to live a legacy-conscious life.

Farmer's Wife as Manager

When I contemplate my mother's legacy, I remember her very full life of work. In those days her role was simply that of a *farmer's wife*. I was reminded of her good management recently when reading Jerry Apps' memoir, *Every Farm Tells a Story*. My sister sent me the book last Christmas, and I quickly realized why.

The story of this Wisconsin farm family closely parallels the story of our own Wisconsin farm family. As was true of the Apps family, the central role of Ma was realized only when illness led to hospitalization. "Ma's illness brought home in a powerful way how farm families depended on each other, especially on the mothers whose work was often taken for granted," writes Apps. "That spring and summer, my brothers and I—and I suspect Pa, too—gained a powerful new appreciation and love for Ma." Her role and responsibilities almost make those of a corporate CEO seem small. She did what was expected of farm women.

> My family depended on Ma more than we knew. She kept the house in order, cooked our meals, washed and ironed our clothes, cared for chickens, and maintained a huge vegetable garden. She kept track of all the farm's expenses and income in her record books. She baked, canned, and traded eggs for groceries during

our regular Saturday-night trips to town. She cooked for the threshing and silo-filling crews, and provided meals for relatives who dropped in at mealtimes expecting something to eat. Ma made sure us boys finished our chores on time. She nursed us when we were sick, helped us with our homework, and always listened when we had a problem or concern. She did this all with a quiet, no-nonsense efficiency.[2]

Here is a personal legacy that parallels the legacy left behind by my mother and by countless other nameless mothers and ordinary individuals through generations of time. What often sets them apart is an ability to manage the necessities alongside the nonessentials—to blend work and play and duty and pleasure together. Management skills serve the individual well. But legacy is surely as much mystery as management. Some people, without even seeming to try, leave incredible legacies.

Writing Mode and Daily Management

My life is a world away from the Wisconsin farm life of my mother's. She would be amazed at how I fit everything in its place—even as I am amazed as I think back on her busy life. But I like to think that my laid-back drivenness is inherited from my mother. She was driven, but she always had time for interruptions. She loved picnics and pranks and playfulness—always finding time for fun amid a heavy schedule. Her legacy inspires me.

Managing my everyday life is often stressful. Even as I write I'm contemplating how I will keep up my writing schedule in the midst of so many other activities and a life that is packed full with family and friends. Every day there is work to do with the grass and shrubs and flowerbeds and vegetable garden, and we set aside time for biking, canoeing, or other exercise. All the while I'm planning for speaking engagements in the coming months. But looming over everything is this book deadline.

How does one write a book in the midst of so many other activities? For me, through the experience of writing more than a dozen other books, the solution has been to go into what I term "writing mode," committing myself to writing an average of one thousand words a day. As with previous books, much of the research is done ahead of time as I'm preparing course lectures. But writing requires a special discipline. So in the midst of an otherwise busy life, I jot down word counts on my calendar: Monday–1,008; Tuesday–656; Wednesday–1,326; Thursday–1,129; Friday–1,438; Saturday–611; Sunday–328; Monday–1,796; Tuesday–1,536; Wednesday–1,029; and by the end of summer, hopefully I will be ready to start preparing the first draft which will be sent on to my editor.

My life-management details are not presented to demonstrate that I am a *leader* and to call others to *follow* me. Rather, I offer them as an example of how I struggle to lay the groundwork for a "well-done" legacy. For most people, life takes a very different course. How one manages everyday life must be designed for specific needs and particular personalities. I am a multitasker who is able to snatch short periods of time for writing. And the menial work of raking and mowing and weeding and house-painting offers time to mull over ideas.

When my friend Sarah from London (of jabberworks.livejour nal.com fame) read about my "writing mode" that I'd posted on a website, she wrote back with her own "mode"—her way of disciplining herself as an artist:

> I really like your latest post; it's fascinating to get an insight into how people actually work, not just see the results. I've found the nerdiest way imaginable to keep working hard. It wouldn't work for writing, and only for certain parts of illustrating. A friend moved back to Australia and left me her BBC Lord of the Rings audio cassettes. I already know the story back to front, and I hardly listen to them while they're playing. But there's something about the pace of the narrative, the fact everyone's striving to fulfill a quest, and having to get up and change the cassettes every hour or so, that makes me plow full steam ahead with my work. I turn into this total work machine. I tried it with other stories. . . . But there's nothing like this particular version of Tolkien to put me on a single-focused frenzy. . . [though] I'm getting very tired of hobbits.[3]

On some days I find writing very difficult, thus the allowance for days with no words at all. And there is no real separation between my writing and my personal life. Today (June 27, 2007) is a particularly difficult day. I always check my email early and am often put in a good mood by a late-night humorous story or an incident sent by Annie. Not today.

Annie's Legacy

Annie has been dear to my heart for many years—beginning in Texas in the 1960s when we were college roommates. She's battled cancer for some years now, but recent word had been good. This morning the message was short:

> After a couple days of feeling really up, I got some bad news today that quickly put me in a down mood. . . . My CAT scan shows 3 more lesions on my liver. . . . That most likely means I will have a much stronger chemo. Oh how I dread that, as so far I have always kept my hair and my nausea has been controllable. I really don't know what to say [I just feel so sad] other than to ask you to pray for me that I can "deal" mentally as well as physically for what is ahead.

It was Annie whose contagious laughter helped me survive a wretched recent employment situation. Her home is always open to us and to a host of other travelers. But far more than that, her heart is open to strangers in need. She has connections across the country and has organized all kinds of homegrown benefits for her "friends" stretching from Katrina-ravaged New Orleans to an Amish community whose children were shot dead in a schoolhouse. Cancer never slowed her down. But today's message seemed more ominous than previous ones.

I had decided as soon as the idea for this book was conceived in my mind—more than a year ago—that it would be dedicated to Annie. She's not what most people would identify as a *leader*—though she certainly has motivated others to join her causes. But she is a model for a well-done legacy that has been growing into a mountain of good deeds over the decades through simple everyday acts of kindness. So today I strive for one thousand words with a heavy heart—though motivated more than ever to get the manuscript to the publisher sooner than later.

Self-Awareness without Self-Absorption

If my everyday management sounds too good to be true, it's not. I have serious problems with organization—and with losing things. My desk is uncluttered at the moment, but my files are not as orderly as they should be.

Nor am I mentally and emotionally invincible as I once thought I was. Eleven years ago is what I speak of as the summer of my mental illness. This too is part of the legacy I will pass on. I was over my head as a general contractor trying to turn a residential property into a commercial property and getting a gift and garden business off the ground. Cost overruns, a hastily planned wedding for my son and his fiancée, an auto accident totaling my van, another car wreck causing the premature birth of a granddaughter, weeks of visiting the neonatal unit every evening—it all took its toll. I was popping a half-dozen Sominex every night, still unable to sleep, and I was described by an asphalt layer as "that skinny lady"—no doubt he used a more colorful name under his breath. I imagined my extreme unhappiness was due to circumstances. I learned only later that I was no doubt clinically depressed, a condition that (as typically happens) just gradually dissipated.

Although this was a very difficult time in my life, I recognize it as a good story with more than a touch of humor. Soon after that painful summer, I was attending a professional conference. I had been avoiding a colleague from another school the entire day, knowing he was going to press me to finish my portion of a project that he had dropped years earlier. I had now moved on to other things and had no time to clean up his mess. But I could tell the way he was talking to others that he was persistent. He cornered me during a coffee break, but I was ready for him. I listened to his pitch and, without sparing words, I responded: "I can't. I'm mentally ill." After he recovered from his momentary shock, he stuttered, "I'm very sorry. I'll find someone else to do it."

Had I responded with any other illness—rheumatoid arthritis or intestinal colitis—he would have persisted to the point of wearing me down. But mental illness is a conversation stopper. And, now thanks to a good excuse from that previous summer of my affliction, I was able to better manage my everyday life without one more project. Everyone has a breaking point, as I was reminded by the *Sally Forth* comic strip today. The summer blahs are overcoming the office, evidenced by expressions and sighs of co-workers. Sally is sitting at her desk benumbed and thinking: *I wonder how high I could count before losing my mind.* What a line. I claim it as my own.[4]

Management of everyday life and legacy involves self-awareness—without self-absorption. I know from personal experience that if there's one way to get off track, it is self-absorption. I've always liked the title of Eugenia Price's book: *Leave Yourself Alone: Set Yourself Free from the Paralysis of Self-Analysis.*

Family and Friends

Legacy is inseparable from relationships. Here family and friends reign supreme. My marriage to John increased very suddenly the size of my little family of one son and one granddaughter. In a moment, I had, in addition to a husband, two stepdaughters and their husbands and three stepgrandchildren. But I knew ahead of time that family would not include the living only. The dearly departed, most specifically Ruth, John's first wife, and Myra, his second, would always have a very cherished place in our family. Their personal legacies are fashioned in intricate ways as John remembers their lives and retells their stories. Their lives and their marriages to John intertwine with our own lives and marriage.

Family life is fragile, as John surely knows—and as I know, having escaped a previous marriage after nineteen difficult years. Families, like friendships, break down. The words of Samuel

151

Johnson are as fresh today as when he wrote them almost three hundred years ago:

> Life has no pleasure higher or nobler than that of friendship. It is painful to consider, that this sublime enjoyment may be impaired or destroyed by innumerable causes, and that there is no human possession of which the duration is less certain.[5]

Friendship is based on trust, and when trust is irrevocably broken, so goes the friendship. One of my books is dedicated to a girlfriend since second grade: "With love and gratitude for forty years of friendship." But only a few years after I had written those words, she put our friendship on the line when she (and especially her husband) relentlessly pressed me to falsely testify in behalf of a fraudulent insurance claim. My initial disappointment turned into anger, and we have not communicated since.

The pain of this loss of friendship may have been exacerbated by my fears of such losses. Perhaps I prize relationships too much. I grew up in a family in which parents and aunts and uncles and cousins became angry and didn't speak to each other—sometimes for years on end. And it has infected my generation as well. What a tragedy when some less-than-pleasant remarks (from both sides) during a short family vacation led to not speaking to each other for four years and counting—despite apologies. But family habits and heritage are hard to break. Again from Samuel Johnson: "Many have talked, in very exalted language, of the perpetuity of friendship. . . . But these instances are memorable, because they are rare."[6]

A Legacy of Faith

My heritage of faith, as with other aspects of the legacy I inherited, is a mixed bag. One beloved minister, I learned years after the fact, was forced to leave the little country church that nourished my faith because of inappropriate relationships with teenage girls. I may have been next on his list. A visiting missionary who had a significant impact on my life was later charged with molesting children at a boarding school in Africa. But this legacy I inherited also included two women. I write about their legacy of faith in *Women in the Maze*:

> The setting was a rural community in northern Wisconsin in the 1930s. Enter two lady preachers—Miss Salthammer and Miss Cowan—convinced that they were called by God to plant a church where there was no gospel ministry. In the years that followed they did just that. . . . Finally when the little church was on solid footing, they moved on to plant other churches.[7]

Years later as I was growing up in the 1950s, they occasionally returned to conduct vacation Bible school. "I thought they were rather odd characters, and it has not been until recent years that I have begun to appreciate them for who they were and for the incredible sacrifice they made." But I was a child. Surely the adults recognized and rewarded their sacrificial legacy. Not so. When "Miss Cowan died, she was buried in a pauper's grave. The county paid for her burial because no one else—not even the people of my little country church—came forward with the money."[8]

Where would I be today were it not for the sacrificial ministry of Miss Salthammer and Miss Cowan? They might have imagined that they would be quickly forgotten. But as long as I live I will seek to keep their legacy alive.

As each one of us is involved in legacy making, we are inspired by the legacies of others. We cherish the memories of the dearly departed as we pass their legacies on to the next generation.

13

JEFFERSON AND JEFFERSON

Walk Like a Man

A recent visit to Monticello reminded me of the incredible legacy of Thomas Jefferson. He was the nation's third president, the one who steered the country toward democratic ideals that had been less pronounced in the administrations of his two predecessors. In 1803 he maneuvered—amidst strong opposition—the largest onetime land acquisition in American history, the Louisiana Purchase. The following year marked the beginning of the Lewis and Clark Expedition. But his service as an American statesman had begun long before his presidency. He served as a colonial legislator, author of the Declaration of Independence, governor of Virginia, minister to France, secretary of state, and vice president. In addition to his government service, he was an inventor, an architect, a musician, a writer, a horticulturist, and an authority in various other fields of interest—all while carrying out his mission of founding the University of Virginia.

Jefferson's reputation as a renaissance man is legendary. Perhaps the greatest nod to his fame came in 1962, when President Kennedy greeted guests at the White House, including forty-nine winners of the Nobel Prize. Kennedy's quip was telling: "I think this is the most extraordinary collection of talent and of human knowledge that has ever been gathered together at the White House—with the possible exception of when Thomas Jefferson dined alone."

If Thomas Jefferson is at one extreme end of the spectrum of success, the person at the opposite extreme is another man (albeit fictional) named Jefferson—no doubt named for the former. The setting is the South of the 1940s—Louisiana, to be precise—where he grew up in the plantation "quarter," a community that was in many ways little different from the slave quarters of a century earlier. The story opens with his trial. He had been charged with being an accomplice in robbing a store and murdering the shopkeeper, an old white man. Though in actuality he was little more than a bystander, the all-white jury finds him guilty and sentences him to death by electrocution.

The narrator is Grant Wiggins, the local schoolteacher for black children, who also grew up in the quarter. Prodded by his aunt who has raised him, Wiggins visits Jefferson in his courthouse jail cell during the months prior to his execution. As their relationship slowly develops, they have an unexpected influence on each other. In the end, Jefferson dies in the electric chair, but not before leaving a profound legacy that speaks to issues of race and gender and family and church and community relationships.

A Lesson before Dying

The two Jeffersons were brought together in my mind in early October of 2007, when I visited the first Jefferson's Monticello estate while I just happened to be reading Ernest J. Gaines's *A Lesson Before Dying*. Though Jefferson is a figment of Gaines's imagination, he became more real to me than the larger-than-life Founding Father of Monticello. I was there in the cell with Mr.

Wiggins when Jefferson raged against his own lawyer and when Miss Emma and Tante Lou begged him to eat from the basket they had prepared and as they pleaded with him to talk with them. I was there when he finally began to open up to Mr. Wiggins and when he walked shackled to the electric chair.

His legacy, however, might be less than obvious to a speed-reader. It slowly unfolds through the pain of those who love him, particularly his nanan, Miss Emma. But the discourse that makes it most transparent comes just two weeks before his encounter with the electric chair. The conversation, prompted by the time of year, has touched on Good Friday and Easter and God and heaven—and how Jefferson fits into the scheme of things. He is finally beginning to comprehend what Mr. Wiggins has been impressing upon him—that he is a man and that he has the opportunity to "walk like a man." He also has the opportunity to inspire—and incite—a whole community, black and white, demonstrating, not only with the dignity, but also the demonic side of human nature. His ultimate realization of his legacy is poignant.

> "I'm the one got to do everything, Mr. Wiggins. I'm the one." He got up from the bunk and went to the window and looked up at the buds on the high branches of the sycamore tree. Through the branches of the tree I could see the sky, blue and lovely and clear. "You Are My Sunshine" was playing on the radio. Jefferson turned his back to the window and looked at me. "Me, Mr. Wiggins. Me. Me to take the cross. Your cross, nanan's cross, my own cross. Me, Mr. Wiggins. This old stumbling nigger. Y'all axe a lot, Mr. Wiggins." He went to the cell door and grasped it with both hands. He started to jerk on the door, but changed his mind and turned back to look at me. "Who ever car'd my cross, Mr. Wiggins? My mama? My daddy? They dropped me when I wasn't nothing. Still don't know where they at this minute. I went in the field when I was six, driving that old water cat. I done pulled that cotton sack, I done cut cane, load cane, swung that ax, chop ditch banks, since I was six." He was standing over me now. "Yes, I'm youman, Mr. Wiggins. But nobody didn't know that 'fore now. Cuss for nothing. Beat for nothing. Work for nothing. Grinned to get by. Everybody thought that's how it was s'pose to be. You

156

too, Mr. Wiggins. You never thought I was nothing else. I didn't neither. Thought I was doing what the Lord had put me on this earth to do." He went to the window and turned to look at me. "Now all y'all want me to be better than ever'body else."[1]

In the end, Jefferson does die for his people. On the Friday of the electrocution, there is a pall over the town—especially the quarter where his people have all taken the day off to show their respect. He dies like a man—a symbol of black dignity that will inspire and incite change. And for the white folks there is a powerful message summed up in one line of Jefferson's halting handwriting in the notebook Mr. Wiggins gave him. He has reflected on eternal matters and comes to what, for all the world, seems like an obvious conclusion: "It look like the Lord just work for white folks."[2] Yes, Jefferson, it does. This is certainly what it looks like as you are counting down the hours in your cell.

The Power of the Pen

Jefferson is a fictional character. But he is real to his creator, Ernest J. Gaines, who passes his legacy on to the black community who all know him and to people like me who can only dimly grasp who he is. Even when we are in the cell with him, we barely comprehend. But he doesn't discriminate. His legacy is for all who will accept the gift.

Ernest J. Gaines grew up in Louisiana in the 1930s and 1940s. "In his childhood, the center of his world was the old slave quarters on the River Lake Plantation, where five generations of his family lived." Like his characters, his "early schooling consisted of six years at the elementary school in the one-room church in the quarters."[3]

Ernest's own legacy as a writer is passed on not only through his several books, all set in Louisiana, but also through his other writings and teaching at the University of Louisiana at Lafayette. His books have been made into films and translated into many languages, and he has won numerous awards. *A Lesson Before Dying* was nominated for the Pulitzer Prize for Fiction; and in

2004, he was nominated for the Nobel Prize in Literature. But perhaps the biggest boost to his writing legacy was when *A Lesson Before Dying* was chosen in 1997 for the Oprah Book Club Selection. Jefferson had gripped the heart of the one considered by some to be the most influential woman in the world, Oprah, who needs no last-name identification.

She understood the racism of the Deep South where she was born and lived her earliest years in neighboring Mississippi. Growing up in Milwaukee, she overcame all odds to excel in school, but then got in trouble as a teenager and was sent to Tennessee to live with her strict father. She won speaking and beauty contests, went off to the university, and became the host of a low-rated talk show. The rest is history. The fictional legacy of Jefferson is passed on to Oprah and makes waves that have a ripple effect around the world.

There is irony in Jefferson and Jefferson and Ernest and Oprah. The first Jefferson, unlike the other three, was born into a culture of significant wealth—a lifestyle of plenty that included not only education and the arts but also a freedom to pursue one's aspirations in life. Such could hardly be said of the other Jefferson. And Ernest and Oprah were forced to overcome incredible obstacles before realizing anything remotely resembling Jeffersonian Democracy.

Legacy of Democracy

Democracy is in some ways the overarching legacy of Thomas Jefferson. But like a deck of cards, democracy had to be played out. Though not a card player (like most other gentlemen from Virginia), he played exceptionally well the hand that life dealt him. He missed the opportunity, however, to play his one remaining card. He waited too long. At the end of the game, the ace of diamonds was still in his hand. Slavery, within the framework of democracy, had not been abolished. As a result, the fictional Jefferson and Ernest and Oprah were dealt cards from a stacked deck—if they were allowed in the game at all.

158

It's not as though Thomas Jefferson had not wanted to play his hand well. He spoke strongly against slavery, proposing slave emancipation in Virginia as early as 1769, when he was still in his midtwenties. Several years later when he was drafting the Declaration of Independence, he denounced the British crown for waging a "cruel war against human nature" through its slave trade, but the condemnation was deleted due to slaveholder opposition. Yet, he pressed on. "The whole commerce between master and slave," he wrote some years later in his *Notes on the State of Virginia*, "is a perpetual exercise of the most boisterous passions, the most unremitting despotism on the one part, and degrading submissions on the other."[4]

Despite his opposition to slavery in his younger years, he accepted the racist convictions of his era—namely, that blacks were inferior to whites and could not live in harmony under the same government. But following his presidency in 1809, he expressed in a letter his willingness to reconsider his views. "My doubts," he said, referring to his belief that blacks were inferior, "were the result of personal observation on the limited sphere of my own State, where the opportunity for the development of their genius were not favorable and those of exercising it still less so." Yet, he did not free his own slaves—with the exception of his five most favored slaves who won their freedom at his death. The remaining slaves were sold to pay his debts. His intention had been to free them when he was debt free, but he never was.

Walking the grounds of Monticello, one is impressed with the incredible architecture and landscaping. The plantation had everything and more for a state-of-the-art home of the early nineteenth century. Modern conveniences are featured in one room after another, and the library he possessed is truly impressive. With Monticello in the rearview mirror, we drove on to the University of Virginia, where Jefferson's legacy of learning lingers today in every classroom and library nook.

He left an astonishing legacy. But what if he had played the ace of diamonds? What if—instead of Monticello and the University of Virginia—Jefferson had focused his impressive wits and energy on abolishing slavery? What if slaves had been freed a full half century earlier than they were? What if the Civil War had never been waged? What if Lincoln were an unknown figure and Jefferson was the president known for freeing the slaves? Life as we know it would be very different.

Money and the Pursuit of Happiness

Money cannot buy happiness easily rolls off our lips. But money can go a long way in the *pursuit* of happiness that Jefferson wrote into the Declaration of Independence as an *unalienable right* that often depends on money. The words are forever lodged in our collective memories: *We hold these truths to be self-evident, that all men are created equal, that they are endowed by their Creator with certain unalienable Rights, that among these are Life, Liberty and the pursuit of Happiness.* But the very freedom of his own slaves was a matter of money. Land and goods might have been sold to purchase their freedom.

Generosity with one's money paves the way for others to pursue economic independence and education and many other *freedoms* that aid in the pursuit of happiness.

As we contemplate legacy and that seal of approval—*Well done, good and faithful servant*—we must consider what we do with the wealth we possess. Thomas Jefferson's wealth depended to a significant extent on slavery. But in the end, his wealth, apart from freeing a few slaves, did nothing to eradicate that system.

Some of the most stirring of the legacy stories are the ones all around us that parallel that of the fictional Jefferson. Jefferson wasn't even a man, his lawyer had said, arguing that he was no more than a hog. How could a reasonable jury convict a hog? In defending his client, he had leveled an affront more stinging than the death penalty itself. But in the end, Jefferson was a man. Not merely three-fifths of a man, as the famous Compromise had called for. His story has inspired millions, as has the story of Ernest Gaines, his creator, and Oprah, his most famous fan. The book title *A Lesson Before Dying* might more appropriately have been *Lessons Before Dying*. Indeed, there are many lessons to be drawn, among them a lesson of giving back to one's community.

Thomas Jefferson, a landed gentleman of great wealth, was deeply in debt when he died. He was unable to free his slaves, much less leave behind a monetary legacy for good causes. Like some wealthy people today, he lived above his means. But there are also many stories of wealthy people who made charitable giving a major part of their living legacy. Such giving is all the sweeter for those who have known poverty and hard times themselves. Among *Business Week's* annual ranking of "America's Top Philanthropists" in recent years has been Oprah, who in 2004 donated more than one hundred and fifty million dollars to various charitable organizations.[5]

She's not alone. Studies show that "a new kind of African American philanthropy is on the rise." But African American giving is not new. It is wrongly assumed that the black community is on the receiving end of charity. Not so. "The African American community doesn't just participate in philanthropy. According to recent studies, it trumps other major racial and ethnic groups in its generosity." Indeed, a recent study showed that "African Americans who give to charity donate 25% more of their discretionary income than whites."[6]

One of the most memorable moments in the life of the fictional Jefferson was when he was specifying individuals—including his white prison warden—who were to receive items from his few meager possessions. Here he is in his cell on the day of his execution thinking of others. Paul, his kindly white warden, tells him he cannot accept the gift of the radio but offers to give it to the other inmates to use in the dayroom. But Paul does accept the gift of a marble. And in response to Jefferson's question, he assures him he will be there with him to the very end—when *it* happens.

In the end Jefferson gave all he had on that sunny afternoon even as the town was brought to a standstill. Folk weren't sure what to say. "Someone asked was it always between twelve and three, and another man said yes, it always was. And someone else said the Lord died between twelve and three on a Friday."[7]

161

A life was taken that day. A legacy left behind: more than anything else, a flickering hope for racial justice and reconciliation. Jefferson's death roused the anger—and sympathies—of both black and white in the story itself. But far more, the story of Jefferson as told in the book and the play performed in theaters around the country has served to change hearts and minds. Thomas Jefferson's words that *all men are created equal* come to life through the death of another Jefferson.

14

THE LEMON FACTOR

Good from Bad

Every culture has its proverbs. One that I heard growing up—one that we all know—is *when life gives you a lemon, make lemonade*. The disagreeable lemon, unlike its orange and grapefruit cousins in the citrus family, is too sour to simply enjoy for its own sake. Peter, Paul, and Mary sang the words: "Lemon tree very pretty and the lemon flower is sweet, but the fruit of the poor lemon is impossible to eat." But what would I do without lemon to flavor the tilapia we had for dinner this evening? For me, lemon on fish is like catsup on a burger. But the lemon stands for "loser" when it comes to cars and appliances—as well as in the lemonade proverb.

It is through this proverb that some unlikely individuals are brought together: a Civil War–era minister's wife, Mrs. Packard; Darryl Hunt, a poor black teenager growing up in North Carolina in the 1980s; Monica Caisons, a teenage runaway involved in drugs and gangs; and Victor Frankl, a Holocaust victim who survived to tell his story and more. They represent countless individuals who drew from the well of misfortune and found treasure for themselves and others. They are neither saints nor superheroes. They are ordinary individuals who were carrying out ordinary functions in the routine of life when they were suddenly faced with a crisis.

Monday means back to work for most people. For an American wife and mother in 1860, it meant wash day. In this era before the wringer washer had been invented, washing was arduous labor. Water was often carried from a nearby river or well and heated over a wood fire. Homemade soap and items of clothing were placed in a large tub, and then the backbreaking job of stirring began. But the daylong ordeal was only getting started. Each item was wrung out by hand and then hung on a line or laid in the grass to dry—unless it was a freezing winter day as was too often the case south of Chicago in the small Illinois town of Monteno.

An "Insane" Mrs. Packard

There would be no washing on Monday, June 18, at the Packard home. The Reverend Theophilus Packard, minister of the local Presbyterian church, was taking his wife Elizabeth, against her will, to the Jacksonville Insane Asylum. She was forty-three and the mother of their six children. Married to Elizabeth for more than twenty years, the authoritarian Theophilus was unable to control her outspoken opinions. She did not agree with his staunch Calvinism, and she did not hesitate to speak her mind. This was not merely a matter of dusty church dogma. Total depravity was a harsh doctrine with very personal consequences— especially in an era of high mortality for little ones who might very well be damned to eternal perdition. This was not, she argued, the law of a loving God. But in her effort to defend God, her little ones were deprived of her own loving care. According to Illinois law, "Married women . . . who in the judgment of the medical Superintendent [of the Jacksonville Asylum] are evidently insane or distracted, may be entered or detained in the hospital on the request of the husband of the woman . . . *without* the evidence of insanity required in other cases."[1]

When she was forcibly taken from her home on that fateful morning, neighbors were shocked and the children were hysterical, but Theophilus was acting within legal bounds. "Illinois law had made him the arbiter of his wife's mental state, God's law made him the guardian of her soul. He was committing her to save her soul, to keep her from endangering the souls of their children, and to shield his creed from her criticism."[2]

Elizabeth had wrongly assumed that the Bill of Rights granted her freedom of religion. She was not after all joining the migration of Mormons to Utah or propagating papal decrees to the children. But she was challenging the very Calvinist dogma that had surrounded her from childhood—and doing so publicly. A submissive, compliant pastor's wife she was not. For a minister's wife to take such a stand today would be controversial. In the spring of 1860, it was downright scandalous. She had her supporters, however, and Theophilus was anything but a popular charismatic community figure. When he sought to stifle her, she blatantly told him she would join with the Methodists in town and take her doctrine with her.

In some respects, Theophilus was caught between a rock and a hard place. There was no Focus on the Family hotline to call. Nor were there other couples modeling good marriages amid strong philosophical and religious differences as we see today. What were his options? Some men might have sought to woo her back to the fold with cuddling and kindness—or with a mixture of scolding and the silent treatment. Theophilus chose conspiracy, dishonesty, and deceit. With his secret plan and the help of others, he laid plans for kidnapping her and removing her from the family for her own good. He had conspired to prove her insane. Insubordinate she was, but surely not insane. He knew this, but his aim was punishing her, and he refused to allow ethics to get in the way. He couched the lie in logic: "Never before had [she] persistently refused my will or wishes . . . she seems strangely determined to have her own way, and it must be that she is insane."[3]

After taking her to the Jacksonville Asylum, Theophilus sought to erase the children's memory of her—though utterly without success. He later complained: "I never saw children so attached to a mother . . . I cannot by any means wean them from her nor lead them to disregard her authority in the least thing. . . . She seems by some means to hold them in obedience to her wishes just as much in her absence as in her presence."[4]

As a mother, I cannot even begin to imagine how Elizabeth survived the ordeal without truly going insane. How would these motherless children survive? Baby Arthur was but a toddler. Though being the homemaker for a large family was grueling work, how she must have longed to be back home on wash day and six other days of the week. Away from home, she remained under the tight control of her husband. "Theophilus forbade the children, whose ages ranged from eighteen months to eighteen years, to communicate with or talk about her. He kept her inherited income from her, deprived her of her clothes, books, and personal papers, and misrepresented her situation to her father and brothers."[5]

During her stay at the institution, Dr. McFarland, in reference to her insanity, wrote that "for two years of the closest study . . . I could [not] discover any intellectual impairment at all, certainly nothing that deserves the name." Later when questioned by a state investigator, he suggested that everyone is at least slightly insane, and referring to her, stated, "There is not one in 1,000 who can possibly detect it. In fact the variation [of insanity] in her case is the slightest there can possibly be." Yet, he kept her confined. Indeed, after she was released and exonerated, he actively worked against her efforts to reform Illinois law. His own reputation was at stake.[6]

Trial by Jury and in the Court of Public Opinion

Elizabeth was released in June of 1863, through the efforts of her sister and her son, who had then turned twenty-one. She returned home but not to freedom. Her husband locked her in the nursery and nailed all the windows shut. This time, however, he had gone too far. Illinois law did not allow a husband to "put away" his wife in her own home. Elizabeth managed to slip a note outside the nursery window. A friend found the note and appealed to a judge for help. The judge issued a writ of habeas corpus (bring forth the body). Now a jury would decide her case—and her sanity.

At the trial, Theophilus called on witnesses to legally prove his wife was insane. Since her biblical and theological views had sent her to the asylum, religious issues served as his primary evidence. He supported his case against her with testimonies from two doctors who had briefly examined his wife on the very morning of her forced departure. Dr. Knott deemed her "partially deranged on religious matters," though he conceded that "on all other subjects she was perfectly rational." Dr. Brown concluded that "she exhibited no special marks of insanity" on domestic matters, but after discussing religion with her—particularly her rejection of the Calvinist doctrine of total depravity—he could say with confidence that he "had not the slightest difficulty in concluding that she was hopelessly insane."[7]

Elizabeth also had witnesses who testified on her behalf. One witness, who was both a physician and a theologian, said he and Elizabeth differed on theological matters but she was clearly not insane. It took just seven minutes for the jury to agree. Elizabeth Packard was a free, sane woman. In the years that followed she became a political activist, publishing her memoirs and traveling to thirty-one states lobbying for legislative reforms. Through her efforts laws and attitudes were changed, and by the time of her death in 1897, her work was internationally recognized.

Although Elizabeth did not have the right to vote, she had been personally penalized by an unjust law. Determined to right that wrong, she spent the rest of her life trying to convince lawmakers to change the laws on mental confinement and women's property rights. The *Chicago Tribune* summed up her legacy in her obituary: "Through the influence of her books, added to her untiring efforts, thirty-four bills have been passed by various legislatures, each benefitting the insane in some way."[8]

Her efforts through the Illinois State legislature to discredit Dr. McFarland as a psychiatrist and insane asylum director failed. In fact, he went on to become involved in the insanity case of a woman more famous than Elizabeth. Mary Todd Lincoln was institutionalized for insanity, and in 1875, her son Robert requested that McFarland examine her with the hope of her being released. He recommended against it and for his services charged Robert one hundred dollars—an exorbitant fee for that era. McFarland had maintained that there was often a fine line between sanity and insanity. His own case might suggest that. In 1891 he hanged himself. He was seventy-four.

Elizabeth is to me a kindred spirit. I too was the wife of a staunch Calvinist minister in a small-town Illinois church. And much of the abuse she suffered I knew all too well. But thanks to Elizabeth and others like her, the laws had changed by the 1970s. Committing me to an asylum was not an option—except the asylum behind closed doors in our home. It was not until 1987 that I escaped with my thirteen-year-old son.

The Trials of Darryl Hunt

Confined to an insane asylum for three years for being a disobedient wife seems like a small price to pay in comparison to being wrongly incarcerated for most of twenty years in a North Carolina prison for kidnapping, rape, and murder. The film *The Trials of Darryl Hunt* tells the story of this innocent man. The victim, Deborah Sykes, was a local newspaper copy editor. Nineteen-year-old Hunt "was just a poor black man who became an easy mark for an array of cynical jailhouse snitches, ruthless criminals, Klan-tinged witnesses and a law enforcement establishment that was anxious to close a terrifying case."[9] DNA evidence finally matched that of another man and proved Hunt innocent. He is not the first to be so exonerated, but the story of his release and freedom is truly singular.

Bitterness might have consumed him and pulled him into a real life of crime. Instead, he used the state damages award to fund a foundation, the Darryl Hunt Project, that helps released prisoners make the transition to life on the streets. What would motivate him to give his award to others? "If you believe in a higher power, then you have to give forgiveness," he insists. "You can't have it just one way, of asking God to forgive you." The non-profit organization has three key objectives: "to provide assistance to individuals who have been wrongfully incarcerated, to help ex-offenders obtain the skills, guidance, and support they need as they return to life outside the prison system, and to advocate for changes in the justice system so innocent people won't spend time in prison." Hunt travels all over the United States speaking out for his cause—and, like Mrs. Packard, challenging legislatures to change discriminatory laws.[10]

For his wrong conviction, Darryl Hunt did not pay the ultimate price of the death penalty. But he knew well that other black men did pay—and not just fictional characters like Earnest Gaines's Jefferson. Hunt fights for justice for such individuals even as he models before them a life of redemption.

Monica and Missing People

In the July 2007 issue of *Reader's Digest* that featured an article on the world's most dangerous leaders, there was another article that related to leadership: "Missing: When People Disappear, Monica Caison Gets the Call." Monica—"this small, chain-smoking, salty-tongued . . . mother of five"—is in many ways the least likely of leaders. She grew up in a family of eleven children in St. Petersburg, Florida. Her mother was a nurse, her father a shoe salesman. "We had the perfect, typical family life," she muses. "No cussing, hair in pigtails, clothes pressed, patent leather shoes." But all that changed when she was eight and her parents divorced, leaving her mother impoverished, living in a crime-ridden neighborhood. "It was roaches on the floor and people breaking in and stealing the little you had every Friday night," she recalls. In fact, she did not resist when she was abducted from school by her father. In the years that followed, she "bounced between parents until eventually a judge awarded custody to her dad." But she repeatedly ran away and at sixteen dropped out of school. Homeless, living on the streets, doing drugs, her life was spinning out of control. Before she was out of her teens, she gave birth to a baby and was arrested and sentenced to jail time for cashing stolen checks. The one thing going for her was the father of her baby—Sam Caison, "a shy, sober, God-fearing boy who adored her despite her wild ways."

> When she was released, she vowed she would turn her life around. She settled down in Wilmington, North Carolina, and married Sam (the father of her baby) who now had a fencing business. In the years that followed, she focused on her growing family of five children. All the while, she volunteered for everything from the PTA to charity drives. It turned out she had a gift for organizing people, and soon she was chairing events at Wilmington's river-front festival, which draws crowds in the tens of thousands. In her spare time, she played drums in an all-girl rock band.[11]

Caison was living the life of a typical soccer mom, until she faced a life-threatening bout with cancer and other serious medical problems. But she was determined to continue giving to others, and in 1994, she found her niche. She led a fund-raising event to support families with missing children. The memories of her own teen years that put her in danger on the streets as well as the fear she saw in the eyes of parents transformed her life. "For as long as she could remember, she had known families ripped apart by sudden disappearances: a childhood friend's mother, another friend's sister, yet another friend's daughter—like Caison in her wayward years—gone AWOL. The idea of helping to repair the damage filled her with an overwhelming sense of purpose."[12]

Soon after, she founded CUE (Community United Effort) Center for Missing Persons. "Before long," writes Kenneth Miller, "she was fielding teams of volunteers to assist in finding teenage runaways. CUE scored some quick successes. But Caison continued to hone her craft, aided by a string of mentors—detectives, dog trainers, even Indian trackers." When she locates a lost person, whether a kidnapped child, a runaway teenager, an addict, or someone struggling with mental problems, "there's no better feeling in the world," says Monica. "I may not be in church on Sunday, but I'm not at home gossiping on the phone. I'm out in the woods—looking for somebody."[13]

The headquarters for the organization is a four-bedroom ranch home where the Caisons live with their five children. Ground zero is a messy office, and the 24-hour hotline is Monica's cell phone. Although CUE oversees a volunteer network of more than seven thousand, the organization is still "very much a one-woman show." Giving her time with no salary, "this small, chain-smoking, salty-tongued and utterly unstoppable mother of five" is philosophical about her mission: "I think God has a plan for everyone's life," she muses, "but people don't always heed what he's trying to show them."[14]

Viktor Frankl's Lessons in Suffering

Viktor Frankl's profound reflections on life come from the black hole of a Nazi death camp, but they apply to all of us in everyday life. For years the sayings of Viktor Frankl have challenged me to live life more fully. "It did not really matter what we expected from life, but rather what life expected from us." Imagine such thoughts coming from one who barely survived the Holocaust. He was practical, with no time for the ivory tower of philosophy or the navel gazing of psychotherapy. "We needed to stop asking about the meaning of life, and instead to think of ourselves as those who were being questioned by life—daily and hourly. Our answer must consist, not in talk and meditation, but in right action and in right conduct." What then is the true meaning of life? "Life ultimately means taking the responsibility to find the right answer to its problems and to fulfill the tasks which it constantly sets for each individual."[15]

I was recently reminded of Frankl through correspondence with one of my online friends. Anna Redsand is the author of *Viktor Frankl: A Life Worth Living* (2006). It's an award-winning young adult book with wonderful pictures that has equal appeal to older adults. She begins the book by identifying him only as prisoner number 119,104 being prodded along wearing only "threadbare rags." Then she relates the story that is best told in his own words. His insights are as moving as they are detailed. Here is what he observed while on a death march to a Nazi concentration camp:

> We stumbled on in the darkness, over big stones and through large puddles, along the one road running through the camp. The accompanying guards kept shouting at us and driving us with the butts of their rifles. Anyone with very sore feet supported himself on his neighbor's arm. Hardly a word was spoken; the icy wind did not encourage talk. . . . Occasionally I looked at the sky, where the stars were fading and the pink light of the morning was beginning to spread behind a dark bank of clouds. But my mind clung to my wife's image, imagining it with an uncanny acuteness. I heard her answering me, saw her smile, her frank and encouraging look. Real or not, her look then was more luminous than the sun which was beginning to rise.
>
> A thought transfixed me: for the first time in my life I saw the truth as it is set into song by so many poets, proclaimed as the final wisdom by so many thinkers. The truth—that love is the ultimate and the highest goal to which man can aspire. Then I grasped the meaning of the greatest secret . . . that the salvation of man is through love and in love. I understood how a man who has nothing left in this world may still know bliss, be it only for a brief moment, in the contemplation of his beloved. . . .
>
> In front of me a man stumbled and those following him fell on top of him. The guard rushed over and used his whip on them all. Thus my thoughts were interrupted for a few minutes. But soon my soul found its way back . . . and I resumed talk with my loved one: I asked her questions, and she answered; she questioned me in return, and I answered. . . . Had I known then that my wife was dead, I think that I still would have given myself, undisturbed by that knowledge, to the contemplation of that image, and that my mental conversation with her would have been just as vivid and just as satisfying.

Frankl was a medical doctor with a specialty in psychiatry when he was incarcerated in a Nazi death camp. He had cut his psychiatric teeth on Sigmund Freud, but soon realized that Freud's basic premise was too simplistic. "At nineteen," Redsand writes, "he saw that psychoanalysis reduced the complexities of being human to a single mechanism . . . that unconscious sexual and aggressive drives dictated human behavior." Even more troubling to him was the fact that the theory could not be tested by scientific methods. Frankl moved on and became a follower of Alfred Adler, who argued that "the need for social superiority was [the] motivating force" for all human behavior. Soon Frankl was challenging that theory and was "expelled from the Society for Individual Psychology because he had criticized parts of Adlerian psychology."[16]

By age twenty-four, Frankl had arrived at his own conclusions—though he insisted he was dwarfed by Freud and Adler. They "were the giants on whose shoulders he had stood to get his firsts glimpses of psychotherapy." His emphasis was in finding the meaning of life, first through meaningful activities (such as one's career or artistic endeavors), second through an encounter (such as kayaking rapids or finding love in relationships), and third through suffering—the "ability to turn suffering into human triumph."[17]

Frankl is my mentor as I contemplate facing life's difficulties and setbacks. He challenges me in my teaching and writing on matters of leadership and legacy. He relates how he repeatedly admonished his students: "Don't aim at success—the more you aim at it and make it a target, the more you are going to miss it. For success, like happiness, cannot be pursued; it must ensue, and it only does so as the unintended side effect of one's personal dedication to a cause greater than oneself."[18]

15

AN EARTHKEEPING LEGACY

Less Is More

In our culture today, we've got this mentality that you send your kids off to school to get a good enough education to get a good enough diploma, to get a good enough job, to pay well enough to work a thousand miles away from home, to accumulate enough money so they can put you in a nursing home when you get old. What I'm looking for is for my grandkids to argue over who gets to spend the day with grandpa.

These are the words of Joel Salatin, an "elder statesman" of the Christian Agrarian movement that combines environmentalism with a love for the land and specifically a love for farming and family.[1]

Salatin's concerns parallel those of Richard Louv. The title of his recent book says it all: *Last Child in the Woods: Saving Our Children From Nature Deficit Disorder*. With all the alarming childhood disorders, why aren't more people concerned with this one? If children are to grow up with a concern for the environment, they must learn to love nature when they are young.

I've always considered myself a conservationist. I planted thousands of evergreen trees as a teenager and have continued my tree-planting habit (on a much lesser scale) with every move I've made. I enjoy camping and hiking and am a regular visitor to American and Canadian national parks. But my concern for the environment pales in comparison to my husband's. When we married a few years ago, life changed in many ways for both of us. For me one of the biggest changes has related to environmentalism. No longer do I rush through the supermarket and grab the laundry detergent with the biggest markdown sign. No longer do I treat my lawn with chemicals. Environmental publications arrive with regularity. Our charitable giving goes not only to church and Christian organizations but also to various conservation groups.

Yet we are part of a collective problem created by ordinary folks like ourselves—and even more so by those who are regarded as leaders. Corporate CEOs are a case in point. The greater one's *leadership* role, the more prevalent is the utilization of private jets, lavish hotel suites, and stretch limousines. Opulent houses and cars and fashion and leisure—all part of leadership prestige— add further to the carbon footprint. Prominent Christian leaders are no different. Or are they? They are perceived to be just as consumer-oriented and wasteful as the leader who makes no profession of faith.

Carbon Footprint

When I mentioned the word *carbon footprint* to a Colorado friend, she rolled her eyes and mumbled something under her breath that I took to mean she was less than impressed with one more *liberal* fad that has been overplayed in the media. But mention the word to others and they respond with a confused look. What is a carbon footprint? Click on carbonfootprint.com for a detailed answer—and for the following paraphrased explanation:

A carbon footprint is a gauge of the impact human activities have on the environment related to the units of carbon dioxide in greenhouse gases. It consists of both the direct and indirect footprint. The primary footprint is the CO_2 that an individual produces, for example, in home heating and gasoline. The secondary footprint is that which is produced for the individual's indirect consumption, as in the cost of shipping toys made in China.

An important way for me to lessen my carbon footprint is to garden and increase my dependency on the local economy. With every meal that I serve with my fresh garden produce, I reduce my carbon footprint ever so slightly—so also with weekly shopping at the local farmers' market. I hang my wash out on the line, and we often cut the grass with our push mower. Mowing and raking the lawn and shoveling the driveway not only diminish noise and air pollution, but they also afford good exercise that doesn't involve driving to a gym to use expensive equipment— each element adding more CO_2 to the environment. Reusing my water bottles and filling them up with tap water strained through a simple filter is a no-brainer. Our compost bin also serves to lower that ever-looming carbon footprint. Among our favorite pastimes are biking and canoeing, easily accomplished without any expenditure of gasoline.

We have discussed these things with our grandchildren. They now know what a carbon footprint is, and we talk about how they can lessen their own, talking as we walk along Abrigador Trail picking up trash. We try to emphasize the positive besides that of saving our planet. We experience together the flavor of fresh garden tomatoes, compared to the hard flavorless ones purchased in the supermarket. And we have them smell our line-hung sheets and pillowcases, hoping they will urge their folks to take up some of these habits. Not every family has space for clotheslines and gardens or opportunities to be part of a cooperative garden. But every family can and should be working together to conserve energy and lessen pollution.

How will Americans and citizens of the world decrease our collective carbon footprint? Leaders like Al Gore and others make a big difference, but in the end, if we choose to save our planet, it will be through collective realization that we can no longer live the *good life* as mindless consumers. Fortunately, some colleges are getting on board, often with students in the lead. This is true for Calvin College, where students from various disciplines are working with professors "to make Calvin a carbon neutral campus." They research behind the scenes and publicly present their findings in forums, proposing "creative strategies to offset . . . campus emissions, strategies that have been carefully scrutinized for their economic, aesthetic and logistical feasibility." Here is the ground floor of something that will reach far beyond this one campus as students graduate and move on.[2]

Tree Musketeers

An earthkeeping legacy, like every other aspect of our legacy, must be an ongoing one that is passed on to our children. But sometimes the situation is reversed when our children lead us in their commitment for earthkeeping. At eight years old Tara Church was a leader. She was a Brownie Girl Scout who was faced with the decision of paper or tin—as in plates for a camping trip. Two natural resources were at stake. Should they try to save water by not washing tin plates during this California drought, or should they try to save trees by not using paper plates? The scouts discussed the pros and cons with their leader, without coming to an easy answer—until Tara suddenly shouted out the solution: "We should plant a tree!" The idea took hold, and together the thirteen scouts planted a tree.

That single act in 1987 was the beginning of a program of local tree planting under the name of the "Tree Musketeers" that won them an invitation to the Reagan White House the following year. In 1990, the group was incorporated and expanded nationally, spurred on by the tenacity of kid volunteers. In 1997, a decade after its inauspicious beginning, the organization had expanded into a "worldwide network of over two million young people" and "One in a Million" was launched. The goal was to "empower a million kids to dedicate a million volunteer hours to planting a million trees by the end of 2000."[3]

Since this early leadership venture of motivating others to follow her in volunteer work, Tara Church has won awards and been active on the national scene as a delegate to various conferences and has earned graduate and undergraduate degrees. Today the single act that began in 1987 has grown into a far-reaching legacy that brings youth volunteers together for earthkeeping activities.[4]

Planting trees should be a high priority for everyone—not just for "Tree Musketeers." I recently read that every American consumes some seventy-five cubic meters of solid wood every year, including paper and all other wood products. I said to my husband, *How can that be?* We began listing paper products, including household goods (tissue, boxed food, etc.), books, newspapers, magazines, printed documents, and mailings of all varieties. *That sure doesn't add up to seventy-five cubic meters*, I insisted. But then we thought of actual wood. We've burned firewood, bought furniture, and added a deck—all just this past year. The previous year we put an addition onto our house, including large amounts of knotty pine car-siding. And with every new home and garage in the neighborhood, the cubic meters add up. "Across the globe, 32 million acres of trees disappear each year for their wood or to make way for urban sprawl or farmlands."[5] On a more positive note, my husband built me a potting shed using the worn and discolored boards he removed from the older portion of the deck. It offered the rustic appearance we wanted, and it added one more item to our growing recycling list.

Community Involvement

Communities are the key. Mayor George Heartwell is leading the green dream in Grand Rapids—seeking among other things ways in which the city might become less dependent on fossil fuels. The matter of recycling alone is a scandal. The term has been around for decades. All good environmentally conscious citizens recycle. Or do they? In Kent County, Michigan, where I live, only about one in five households recycles. Instead, we dump into landfills and incinerators vast amounts of materials that could be recycled—for a profit—and made into new products.[6] Last night we talked about recycling with friends who had come over for burgers and hiking. We can't save the country, but we can do things to challenge those living around us to recycle their waste.

But not all recycling helps the environment. Years ago when I did my shopping I took my plastics, paper, and glass trash and deposited them in the proper bins located at the back parking lot of a nearby supermarket. But without consulting me, local officials began a pay-to-recycle program that allowed homeowners to put their recyclables on the curb. I felt guilty about not paying up—until I read an article claiming that such recycling does more harm than good. Better to put such recyclables in the trash for pickup day than have extra trucks guzzling fossil fuels and spewing carbon monoxide into the neighborhood. In our haste to be environmentally conscious, we sometimes thwart our noble purpose.

One of the most important ways for communities to consciously deal with environmental problems is to "think small." Indeed, that is one of the ways Youngstown, Ohio, is facing its decline. "For decades the city tried to stem the number of people moving away. Then, city planners decided to take a different approach—accept being smaller and clear away clutter." Such a program involves thoughtful management—not necessarily the kind of *leadership* that seeks to move up to the governor's mansion and on to the White House. "American culture is one of largess," observes Joe Schilling, an urban researcher and professor at Virginia Tech, "so it's hard for any mayor to have to run for office and then say to the voters, 'I think we have to shrink our city.' It sounds like retreat."[7]

The Youngstown plan caught the attention of Jennifer Vey, a senior think-tank researcher for the Brookings Institution: "I don't know that there are many other cities in the country taking such an aggressive approach to managing population shrinkage."

179

However, other cities indeed are taking note. "Being smaller isn't all that bad," a Saginaw, Michigan, official commented, "if you create a quality environment." The emphasis in Youngstown is on opening up more green space and city parks, and there is a spirit of optimism where once there was only a sense of defeat.[8]

Green Church

I was recently asked to contribute material on megachurches for an article to be published in the *Congressional Quarterly*. My book, *Left Behind in a Megachurch World*, had caught the attention of the author who told me in a phone conversation that she was looking for someone who would challenge the whole concept of a megachurch. In an effort not to sound wishy-washy—or to avoid being *nuanced* as the more sophisticated would say—I wrote the following opening paragraph:

> Megachurches are a blight on the landscape of America—as physical structures and as authentic expressions of religion. Their sprawling campuses beyond the suburbs that consume vast tracks of land are comprised of buildings and parking lots that are put to full use only one day a week. They draw worship-goers who drive their SUVs dozens of miles each way. Their large auditoriums utilize air-conditioning, heating, and other utilities far beyond normal per capita use. Their tax-exempt status is supported by all of us. Show me the megachurch that is green.

That last sentence grabbed my attention. (I write fast, and sometimes I surprise myself.) Yes, *show me the megachurch that is green.* Is it possible for a megachurch to be green? Do megachurches even think in terms of being green? I cannot answer those questions, but each question led me further down the path of contemplating *green* churches.

I grew up in a little green church, though the *Green* Grove Alliance church was actually clothed in white clapboard. But it was *green* before it was cool to be *green*. It was a neighborhood church—no gas-guzzling Hummers coming from miles away. Air-conditioning was provided by open windows on sultry summer Sundays, and the wood furnace kept us warm in winter. Outhouses were available for anyone getting the urge during a long-winded sermon, and the grass was kept trim by a push mower. No PowerPoint presentations or complicated music systems. Flannel-graph stories and an out-of-tune piano served us well.

So much for nostalgia. But is it not time to abandon (or at least stop building) the massive megachurch campuses and return to the greener neighborhood churches? Many of those who drive great distances to attend a Sunday show were once involved in a nearby church. Their presence would help revive this left-behind church, and their challenge could help the church to become *intentionally* green. Evangelicals have a reputation for being out of touch in regard to social movements—or in some cases bringing up the rear. Indeed, it was decades after the civil rights movement before evangelicals in large numbers began talking about the *sin* of racism. And evangelicals could hardly be accused of being out front in the matter of earthkeeping.

Is not the time right for vast numbers of evangelicals to waken from their slumber and say enough is enough? *We are done with this fad of megachurches. We're going to walk to church or ride a bike or grab a subway or drive a few miles to the little green church in the vale.* There are many ways for Christians to become intentionally green, the most deliberate of which is to reclaim—and recycle—neighborhood churches.

Fortunately, leaving behind a legacy of a *green* church is not a matter of reinventing the wheel. Organizations like Interfaith Power & Light offer ideas for lessening the carbon footprint of a local church. "Houses of worship, it turns out," writes Jane Lampman, "are some of the biggest wasters of energy on a per capita, per hour-of-use basis." But what changes the minds of parishioners and church boards is the cost effectiveness:

> Congregations that practice environmental stewardship can save 30 percent on their utility bills, says the US Environmental Protection Agency. If all US congregations did the same, they'd save an estimated $573 million annually and prevent 6 million tons of CO_2 from polluting the air—the equivalent of taking 1 million cars off

the road. . . . By installing solar panels on the roof and changing lighting, Christ Church in Ontario, Calif., saw its summer utility bills drop from $600 to $20 a month. All Saints Episcopal Church in Brookline, Mass., which installed a new boiler with zoned heating, programmable thermostats, and more efficient lighting, was rewarded with annual savings of $17,000. They've used 14 percent of the savings to buy 100 percent renewable energy, further reducing pollutants. Hebron Baptist Church in Dacula, Ga., revamped its lighting system, converting fixtures and exit signs. They're saving $32,000 a year in church expenses and 450,000 kilowatt hours of energy.[9]

Carbon-Footprint Coffin

The news of Ruth Graham's death in June of 2007 was expected, and stories of her life and service were published in newspapers across the country. What caught my eye was a short fifteen-line column in an "In Brief" section with the following words: "Reflecting her simple tastes, a casket built of plywood carried Ruth Bell Graham through the streets of her home in the Blue Ridge range Saturday. . . . The coffin was chosen after son Franklin noticed inmates at the Louisiana State Penitentiary building the caskets for themselves and others who could not afford regular coffins."[10]

My first reaction was to wonder why such a story came in such a tiny brief. I've never heard of this being done before. Ruth Graham is a household name. Shouldn't "plywood coffin" merit a headline just by its singularity? My second reaction was to broach the subject with my husband, who was tinkering with a plumbing problem. It was a simple and straightforward idea. Let's start a "Plywood Coffin" movement. Taking a cue from Ruth Graham, we would make arrangements to be buried in a plywood coffin.

My husband John's role is always that of challenging my wild and crazy ideas—though this was clearly not *my* idea. A precedent had already been set by the saintly—and less than wild and crazy—Ruth Graham. As for me, I've never been a fan of pricey funerals. My frequent throwaway line for many years has been, *Just put my body in a Hefty bag and leave it on the curb.* But now I am dead serious. Less is more when it comes to burial. The example set by Ruth Graham is one I am determined to follow, and in the meantime I will seek to bring others along.

Perhaps I'm jumping into this concept too quickly, but that's my style and it is a good way of testing the waters. On day one, after reading the newspaper brief and making further online inquiries, I've already made several advances: my blog, "Plywood Coffins," is launched, with the purchase of plywoodcoffins.com for $8.84. I also made a phone call to Memorial Alternatives in Grand Rapids (which I've also linked to my site) that offers very inexpensive funerals and is willing to use plywood coffins. I called a local private cemetery where we own plots and learned that there are no regulations prohibiting such a coffin; their concern is the concrete vault, required at all cemeteries. We've also shared the concept with Bruce and Becka, friends up the street who thought it was a great idea. Now the real test is commandeering people who are still breathing to join up and come along with us on this road to the grave.

Paying Rent with Lady Bird

"Her Legacy Shows in Wildflowers" was a headline in the newspaper. Lady Bird Johnson died in the summer of 2007, at age ninety-four. Like my mother, she was born in 1912, attended a one-room country school, and loved wildflowers. But Lady Bird's love of nature was taken all the way to the White House, where her influence as First Lady has been felt in the decades since.

While traveling with her husband in the 1964 presidential campaign, she was distressed to see roadsides cluttered with billboards and litter and junkyards that, according to LBJ, were "driving my wife mad." Indeed, she was so mad that she vowed she would make a difference. Less than a year after her husband was elected president, the Highway Beautification Bill was signed—largely due to her lobbying. Her commitment to the environment continued long after her years at the White House and after her husband's death. In fact, when she was seventy, she founded (with actress Helen Hayes) the National Wildflower Research Center in Austin. When she was asked by reporters why she helped establish the center, she said it was her way of "paying rent for the space I have taken up in this highly interesting world."[11]

Two years ago, while fulfilling a speaking engagement in Austin, my husband and I explored the various sites associated with Lady Bird and Lyndon Johnson. We wanted to see for ourselves the wonderful hill country that they called home. One of my souvenirs was a colorful children's book, *Miss Lady Bird's Wildflowers*. The story begins: "Deep in the heart of Texas lives a woman who loves flowers. 'Wildflowers,' she says, 'are the stuff of my heart!'" The book ends with the same metaphor:

> Now whenever you travel through the countryside and you see a field of wildflowers, be sure to wave to them as you drive by. Learn their names—the lady's slippers, black-eyed Susans, larkspurs, winecups, blazing stars, Granny's nightcaps. As you pass by, call out, "Thank you, Miss Lady Bird!" And remember that it hasn't always been this way. These flowers are ours to keep. They're ours to tend. They're the "stuff of our hearts."[12]

The notion of "paying rent" through beautification on this wonderful space we call Earth is one that ought to challenge all of us who consider ourselves earthkeepers.

Lady Bird played a role in more than two hundred environmental legislative initiatives. As one reporter commented, she was green before it was cool to be green. She serves as a role model not only for children but also for all who desire to leave a legacy of a more beautiful and healthy earth.

16

SMILE WHEN I'M GONE

A Legacy of Laughter

To leave behind laughter. What an incredible legacy. How easy it is to smile as we think back on George Burns or Johnny Carson. I reminded my husband the other day of Red Skelton, and we both began repeating the punch lines of his Clem Kadiddlehopper skits. We wracked our brains to think of Christian comedians who made us laugh. "I know Jewish comedians," he commented, "but Christians don't make good comedians. They take everything too seriously."

But should laughter really be considered a significant element of legacy? We overlook its potency to our peril. Indeed, the influence of political cartoons and the late-night comedians is incalculable—especially in the cultural and political realm. But for ordinary folks, an ongoing legacy of laughter makes the daily grind and the downside of life so much more bearable. And laughter is a treasure passed on freely to friends and family even when the estate and other assets are small. I have wonderful memories of my mother's sense of humor—not so my father.

And when I remember my dear friend Alan Neely, our frequent gales of laughter bring back priceless memories. What a legacy to leave behind.

Laughter and humor are high priorities for me—in my day-to-day life and in my writing. A number of my books take humor into account. *Left Behind in a Megachurch World* has a chapter entitled "Left Behind with a Sense of Humor." "The Humorous Side of Motherhood" is the title of one of the chapters in *Seasons of Motherhood*; and *Family Album: Portraits of Family Life Through the Centuries* features cartoons and humorous anecdotes alongside serious matters. As I'm now contemplating the completion of a church history text, I am making mental notes to include a cartoon or humorous quote or funny story in every chapter. It's a book with a biographical flow—a book that seeks to draw people into the fascinating story of our colorful Christian heritage. A touch of humor will serve the topic well.

For a *left-behind* church, humor is essential, and what a legacy a pastor can offer a church through humor—whether a sense of humor or recognition of humor in others. The minister must be a *leader*, so says the church-growth literature. Without *leadership* the church will die. But what about humor? It is critical, as I write in *Left Behind in a Megachurch World*:

> The *gift* of humor is truly a much underrated "spiritual gift." There is so much talk these days (and in days past) about *identifying one's spiritual gifts* as though such identification automatically paves the way for utilizing such gifts to transform the individual or the church. Most *gifts*, such as those of humor, are obvious. Everyone knows it if the pastor has a quick comeback or a hearty laugh or a dry sense of humor or is one who does not take himself or herself too seriously. And if the congregation is so fortunate to see this in their pastor, they are blessed. There is so much anger, angst, hostility, and fear that can be quickly dispelled by humor. How much better board meetings are when a little humor is employed. The same goes for the building committee and the pleas for more funds. Laughter truly is the best medicine. This *gift* was given to one species only. . . . We often utterly fail to recognize its importance in the matter of church health.[1]

Humor and Memory

There is an important link between legacy and laughter. Legacy and memory are inextricably tied together, and scientists have discovered that memory and laughter have a close connection. After reviewing scientific studies and other literature, Dan Ferber makes the case that "humor can improve memory"—a hunch on which advertisers have operated for decades. The funny TV commercial is the one viewers remember. But now clinical studies have shown that virtually any information, if framed in a humorous way, is more memorable than that which is serious. Ron Berk, statistics professor and psychologist at Johns Hopkins, utilizes this knowledge in his classes through the use of skits and gags and jokes of all kinds. He has published his findings that indicate laughter aids in learning. "Even funny test directions helped students do significantly better on an otherwise identical exam." Ferber is quick to point out that he is not saying "regular helpings of jokes or Adam Sandler movies will qualify us all for Mensa," but a wide range of studies show that memory and laughter are closely connected.[2]

I know this through experience. After church on the first Sunday of the month, we gather to eat our potluck noon meal with John's siblings at Mom's apartment or one of our own homes. Remembering times gone by is a natural theme of our conversation, and the stories that are triggered most often are ones that are funny. And these are the ones that ninety-three-year-old Franny remembers most easily. We especially enjoy those unforgettable stories when things went wrong. Our own wedding is an example. Amid all the preparations, we forgot to buy shrimp cocktail (for the pre-wedding family get-together), which set in motion a comedy of errors that at the time did not seem funny at all. Getting married is serious business. But now, what we remember the most are the things that went wrong—those things that bring us gales of laughter. In fact, we have learned to recognize such stories right in the middle of our angst. We take stock of what is happening and are often able to say, *Well, at least it will make a good story.*

Years ago I was a victim in a purse-snatching incident. It was most unpleasant. I had gone to my bank on Friday afternoon to *deposit* money (when others commonly bring in their paychecks and walk out with cash). The lanky young man presumably thought I looked like I had a purse full of twenty-dollar bills. I didn't. I had five dollars and change, but far more important to me, three videotapes that I would be using for an adult education class. I ended up teaching the class without the video clips, but the story (that I shared with the class) of my giving chase to the thief and the ensuing comedy was worth the price of the purse and its contents. No thief should get off scot-free. But if he does, he deserves to find his take to be little more than three videos of taped TV documentaries on religion.

How sad when that lightheartedness is missing. It has the power to negatively affect our legacy. I recall a solemn installation service some years ago. From beginning to end it was perfectly choreographed—and very stressful. Perhaps to ease the tension, many of those in attendance found an unexpected ray of humor in what they imagined they were seeing in a piece of abstract art. The laughter lightened and brightened the moment—especially during the reception and following days. The honored "celebrity," however, did not see it that way, and for those who had laughed, there was hell to pay. But when we laugh at ourselves and encourage lighthearted humor in the midst of all that is serious, memory is sharpened both in ourselves and in others.

This is actually hard science. Humor (or laughter) is most often produced by *incongruity*—that which happens when our brains see something (as in the piece of art) that is not supposed to be there or when the punch line reverses what is normally expected. We exercise our brain muscles by seeing and hearing such incongruities. And such humorous incongruities in life sharpen our brains and help us process the big problems and incongruities of life. Neuroscientists have discovered (through the use of brain scanners) that those who have a "damaged right prefrontal cortex" (and those who for other reasons never exercise that cortex— perhaps due to a damaged psyche), found humor in slapstick but not in the "so-called thoughtful forms of humor."[3]

Part of this ongoing legacy of laughter is to prepare ourselves for the downturns in life. Back when I was a single mother of a teenaged son, I used to keep ever before me a little motto for life: *Happiness is lowered expectations.* There are others with a humorous touch that have also served me well:

- Just accept the fact that some days you're the pigeon, and other days you're the statue.
- Don't always try to be first. Remember, it's the second mouse that gets the cheese.
- When everything is coming your way, you're probably in the wrong lane.
- Happiness is the ability to enjoy the scenery on a detour.

Cultural Wit and Humor

My husband and I team teach CALL courses (Calvin Academy for Lifelong Learning) on various topics, including one on American Wit and Humor. While researching and teaching the course, we were reminded time and again of the connection between humor and legacy. In our first session we reflected on humor that has lasted through the centuries, beginning with medieval street dramas. One such "mystery play" has Noah nagging his wife to get into the ark, and she refuses to be separated from her gossips. Noah takes a stick and hits her over the head. Such is high hilarity for the medievals. Geoffrey Chaucer's fourteenth-century *Canterbury Tales* serves as another example of medieval humor. In "The Miller's Tale," a carpenter marries a young girl named Alison, but soon she is up to no good with the resident cleric, Nicholas. The tale deteriorates into bawdiness, but the legacy of Chaucer and his tales continues to this day.

Most Protestants simply weren't very funny. Where is the humor in John Calvin or John Bunyan or Jonathan Edwards? Martin Luther was an exception, however. Indeed, his humor softened his sometimes vicious tirades against the pope or even his fellow Reformers. Often his humor was biting and, shall we

189

say, off-color. But like his medieval ancestors, his primary source was the Bible. The flood story was his favorite. For example, he questioned, with a twinkle in his eye, whether "manure was kept on the lowest deck of Noah's ark or tossed out the window."

The main focus of our first CALL course session was Ben Franklin, remembered as much for his humor in *Poor Richard's Almanac* as for his inventions, nation-building, and diplomacy. Our second session featured Mark Twain, but our introductory material included Abraham Lincoln whose humor served him well as a lawyer and politician, and later during the painful war years of his presidency. He was quick with a retort, especially to criticism. When he was accused of being two-faced, he said: "If I had two faces, do you think this is the one I'd be wearing!" Lincoln's great rise from poverty to the presidency was spurred by his lighthearted self-deprecation. Soldiers sometimes magnify their feats of bravery. Of his military service in the Black Hawk War, he shrugged that he had made many "charges on wild onions" and had "a good many bloody struggles with the mosquitoes." When people poked fun of his lanky build, he quipped that a feller's legs needed to be plenty long enough to reach the ground.

Lincoln had a storehouse of canned jokes. His genius was in calling them forth with the timing of a seasoned comedian. Frequently these stories were drawn from the Bible, as in the story of the little boy at a backwoods school. He always blundered when taking his turn to read aloud in class—most notably over the biblical passage of Shadrach, Meshach, and Abednego. When his turn was approaching, he again saw the names before him. He set up a wail: "Look there, marster—there comes them same damn three fellers again!" As Lincoln told the story, he stood at a window overlooking Pennsylvania Avenue and he pointed to three men—blowhard politicians—on their way to the White House. They were Sumner, Stevens, and Wilson: here "comes them same damn three fellers again."[4]

Even the terrible news from the war front was seasoned with humor. In despair and frustration over the progress of the war, Lincoln commented one day that he sure wished he knew what brand of whiskey it was that his successful General Ulysses S.

Grant guzzled so freely. If someone would tell him, he would send a barrel to every one of his generals.

But when it comes to a legacy of laughter, Mark Twain ranks above all others. Like so many before him, his favorite topic was biblical humor. In reference to Methuselah and other centuries-old biblical characters, Twain asked: "Now, why—why will a man, when he gets to be a thousand years old, go on hanging around the women, and taking chances on fire and brimstone, instead of joining the church and endeavoring, with humble spirit and contrite heart, to ring in at the eleventh hour, like the thief on the cross? Why?"[5]

Mark Twain is far more than a mere humorist. He is a storyteller with few equals, whose influence extends into the twenty-first century.

Garrison Keillor

Today's greatest storyteller, bar none, is Garrison Keillor whose ongoing legacy is far greater than people might imagine. He is a man who models leadership even as he presents himself as an anti-leader. Indeed, he defies any notion of leadership, even in the midst of the ultimate *leadership* surroundings of Manhattan, where he formerly had his office, the setting of Gordon Mac-Donald's interview:

> When Keillor is not entertaining an audience, he is often found in an unpretentious set of offices located on Manhattan's Lower West Side. Papers and posters are piled high; furniture is metal; and staff assistants wear jeans. Keillor in a personal conversation is like Keillor on the radio: low-key, almost embarrassed by the attention, and always thoughtful. Pondering a question, he shoves paper clips or pencils from side to side on his desk. Eye contact is poor; his broken sentences make him sound bored. But when it's time to bring a point to closure, he looks up, a grin spreads across his broad face, and he offers a witty observation.[6]

For decades *A Prairie Home Companion* has captivated fans like John and myself. On Saturday nights we often sit by the radio and laugh until our sides split. "Keillor, with horn-rimmed glasses and an almost boyish face, speaks softly in a halting, unprofessional style," observes MacDonald, "that reminds one more of family supper-table talk than mass entertainment. Keillor fans love it; the show appears to mock the slick, fail-safe kind of show business to which most Americans are accustomed."[7]

Yes, mocking slick, fail-safe show business, and surely the business of *leadership*. The very dead-pan persona is a panning of people who take themselves and their place in life too seriously, imagining themselves more important than they are. Keillor, however, is dead serious about the message he passes along. His book *Home-Grown Democrat* is a plea for people to take their faith seriously as they consider political issues. Here he calls the Democratic Party to recognize its foundational Christian values of helping those in need and caring for the environment.

While unconsciously panning *leadership* in word and style, Keillor draws from a deep family legacy and passes on his own legacy, especially in matters of religious faith. When asked if it was difficult to leave his religious roots, he responded seriously, though always with a touch of humor: "We're talking about a considerable passage of time . . . [more] than moving from a farm to the city . . . a difference between a child and a man." The God of younger years was "always looking." Worse yet, it was not just God with the penetrating gaze: "But also your dead relatives are out there; they're watching." But as he matured he could not "endure the gaze of that God and live." Such a penetrating gaze is insufferable.

> You have to put that merciless gaze out of your mind or you would become a nut living in a mobile home at the end of a long dirt road with his cats, sitting out there eating acorns. Against that pitiless gaze is the vision of Christ the Shepherd with which we also grew up. And there's the miraculousness of the gospel, which you learn more and more about as you get older. After a long lapse, after a long absence, you come back. I came back. And the pitiless gaze is gone somehow.[8]

SMILE WHEN I'M GONE

When the merciless gaze of God is gone, humor can flow freely, as Keillor has discovered. His autobiographical storytelling draws heavily from the religious upbringing he inherited. He seizes the legacy, rather than rejecting it. Like a carnival balloon, he twists and fashions it—and we all laugh as he does it. As an adolescent boy titillated by pictures in *High School Orgies*, a forbidden magazine, he is feeling the pitiless gaze of God:

I am going to spend eternity in hellfire for what is twitching in my mind right now.

Here I am in my room, weeping for my carnal sins, on a warm summer night, and what if the Second Coming is scheduled for nine-fifteen P.M. Central Time and in exactly five minutes the saved of earth will rise into the stratosphere and I will find myself left behind with the heathen?

This could be the case. What if I tiptoe downstairs *right now* and Daddy isn't lying there on the daybed listening to the Millers on the radio—what if all the Sanctified Brethren have whooshed up to the sky, Sugar and Ruth and Al and Flo and LeRoy and Lois, and I am left behind with the Catholics and the atheists and the drunks at the Sidetrack Tap?[9]

Keillor took hold of his legacy and is passing it on to future generations. How sad that so many Christians cling to the pitiless gaze while allowing the legacy of laughter to pass them by.

Smile When I'm Gone

A legacy of laughter is part of a broader legacy of lightheartedness that must be an ongoing aspect of life. Just read the paper or turn on the television news. Serious issues and sadness reign supreme. John and I naturally find fun in our daily routines, but we've also learned the art of not taking ourselves too seriously. So often, right in the middle of bickering, one of us realizes how trivial the matter is and we burst out laughing. Even amid tragedy, we find space for lightheartedness. I'll never forget laughing at Kimberly's funeral. She is forever eleven years old and her sudden accidental death was an indescribable heartbreak. But

Kimberly left behind a legacy of laughter—through letters and notes and funny stories—remembered at the funeral and in the years since.

Will I leave behind a legacy of laughter? The last paragraph of my book, *Seasons of Motherhood: A Garden of Memories*, was written with this topic in mind twelve years ago to my son, Carlton:

> When I am gone and you are left alone, I know your heart will ache and the tears will fall. . . . But when you weep, just remember you are weeping for yourself. . . . But when you smile and laugh and sing and dance, you smile for me; you laugh for me; you sing and dance for me. When you celebrate the joy of life, think of me. And don't ever forget the happy times and the good times we have had together . . . our very own garden of memories.[10]

John has endured the sorrow of losing two previous wives to cancer. But his memories of them are closely tied to good times and laughter. It was a cold January day when his beloved second wife, Myra Jean, was laid to rest. What did he do to pass the time later that afternoon? He took his three grandchildren out in the snow to play and to laugh and to squeal and have a good time. Exhausted, he fell backwards in the snow, the kids following suit, not realizing that Papa, amid all the fun, was making a snow angel for his dear angel Myra in heaven.

17

TENDER MERCIES

A "Cup of Cold Water" Legacy

I was standing in line with my carry-on bags in terminal K at O'Hare preparing for the last leg in our flight from Palm Springs to Grand Rapids. I was tired after two days filled with speaking sessions, a magazine interview, and people wanting to talk. The July daytime temperatures had soared to 112 degrees, and I was eager to get home to the cool 80s of West Michigan. But as I was about to board, I was pulled aside and informed that I would have to spend the night in Chicago and return home the next day because of FAA weight restrictions. I protested: Why was I being singled out? And why was there no travel award for my inconvenience? You were the last person to book your flight, the agent snapped.

As it turned out, a man by the name of Cody was a no-show, and I, after being held back to the very end, was allowed to fly in his place. But I was cranky as I made my way (with husband John) to 18C, in the last row of this American Eagle aircraft. It didn't help my mood that a woman across the aisle was hysterically pleading with the flight attendant to help her. From what we soon learned, she was a first-time flyer, very fearful of flying, had already been on several legs of her journey from Saigon, had been bumped off her flight from Dallas to Grand Rapids, and was now in Chicago fearing she would never arrive at her destination. She didn't speak English, but her tone of voice and body language spoke volumes. The flight attendant tried to reassure her but seemed frustrated by the language barrier, and she had other matters to attend to.

That was when I noticed the young woman sitting ahead of her, reaching back and holding her hand and patting her leg and in a calming voice, nodding, and looking at her ticket and saying again and again, "It's okay. Everything will be all right." Through the flight she continued to hold this woman's hand, and she held her close as they got off the plane and talked with a ticket agent.

As I saw this young woman help a stranger, I was forced to ask myself if I would have done the same had I not been delayed in boarding the flight. I'm not sure. Although I expressed my appreciation to this young woman, she will never know that she may have helped me far more than she helped this distressed stranger. As I think of her, I am reminded of Mitch Albom's book, *Five People You Meet in Heaven*. It is a fictional work about eighty-three-year-old Eddie, the longtime maintenance manager at Rudy Point Amusement Park. The story has a lot of twists and turns, but an important aspect of the book relates to five people in heaven who it turns out—unawares to him—had a significant influence on his life.

Albom's story is the reverse of what we sometimes imagine will happen in heaven—that we will reveal to various people how they had a significant influence on us. If I meet this young woman who was on American Eagle flight 4279, I will again express my gratitude. She is an example of a fleeting legacy that has a ripple effect—reaching out to a stranger and in the process leaving a legacy with another stranger who just happens to notice. And perhaps my recounting this story will have its own legacy ripple effect.

Is this part of what Jesus had in mind with his promise of "Well done, good and faithful servant"? A well-done legacy is one that not only includes the enormous sacrifice of a Mother Teresa but also the tender mercy of giving a cup of cold water to someone who is thirsty. Indeed, a well-done legacy may be no more than an accumulation of tender mercies—little mercies that touch the heart of the one at the receiving end.

I write a bimonthly column for *Plain Truth* magazine entitled "Tender Mercies." My first column made reference to the old hymn that we sang in church when I was a child: "There Shall Be Showers of Blessing." It speaks of wanting to hear the "sound of abundance of rain." The final words of the chorus are "Mercy drops 'round us are falling, but for the showers we plead." My response was, "I think we easily set ourselves up for failure when we are pleading for showers, while ignoring the *mercy drops* that are falling all around us."

In discussing the concept of tender mercies with my husband, he shared the tender mercy that has meant the most to him. When his late wife Myra Jean was being treated for pancreatic cancer, there was always the hope that there would be a breakthrough cure that would spare her life. It was a hope for "abundance of rain." The rain did not come. After living with cancer for almost five years, the end came quickly. For more than a day she lay in a coma. Family and close friends came to the condo to say their good-byes, but she gave no response. It was late in the day. John was alone with her, sitting on the bed holding her hand and whispering comforting words. Then came the tender mercy. No memorable final words. Just squeezing his hand three times. This mercy drop was her final good-bye, forever part of her legacy.

Gilead's John Ames

It is not uncommon for people to contemplate their legacy as death draws near. So it was with the fictional Reverend John

Ames. In the bestselling novel *Gilead* by Marilynne Robinson, the elderly minister knows his days are numbered. He is in very poor health and he is writing down his memories to leave as a legacy for his young son. Some of the stories he records are landmarks, but mostly they are tender mercies:

> A few days ago you and your mother came home with flowers. . . . You had honeysuckle, and you showed me how to suck the nectar out of the blossoms. You would bite the little tip off the flower and then hand it to me, and I pretended I didn't know how to go about it, and I would put the whole flower in my mouth and pretend to chew it and swallow it . . . and you'd laugh and laugh and say, No! no! no!! . . . and then you got serious and you said, 'I want you to do this.' And then you put your hand on my cheek and touched the flower to my lips, so gently and carefully, and said, 'Now sip.' You said, 'You have to take your medicine.' So I did, and it tasted exactly like honeysuckle, just the way it did when I was your age and it seemed to grow on every fence post and porch railing in creation.[1]

Here is a child in one of summer's fleeting moments offering a tender mercy to his father, and his father passing that same tender mercy back to his son in the form of a legacy.

Gilead does not take the reader to the next generation. We have no way of knowing what impact the father's memoirs would eventually have—if any at all. Is the son inspired by the legacy his father bequeathed him? Often in life seemingly insignificant acts leave a mark far beyond their apparent import. And many times these tender mercies fall like drops of rain on children like they did on C. S. Lewis.

A Garden Precursor of Narnia

One summer day during C. S. Lewis's carefree childhood before his mother died, his older brother fashioned a miniature toy garden on a biscuit tin. In it young Lewis saw a tiny secret and sacred space where he pictured himself shrunk down to fit this magical world of moss and twigs. It was an imaginary setting that would evolve into Narnia in his classic work, the Chronicles of Narnia.

> It made me aware of nature—not . . . as a storehouse of forms and colors but as something cool, dewy, fresh, exuberant. . . . As long as I live my imagination of Paradise will retain something of my brother's toy garden. . . . It is difficult to find words strong enough for the sensation which came over me; Milton's "enormous bliss" of Eden . . . comes somewhere near it. . . . It had only taken a moment of time; and in a certain sense everything else that had ever happened to me was insignificant in comparison.[2]

For C. S. Lewis, the life-changing recognition of joy and the origins of the mythical land of Narnia came by way of a biscuit tin—one of life's momentary unexpected tender mercies.

Children play an important role in passing on a legacy of tender mercies. A child does not have the wherewithal to serve as mentor or as a patron for an artist or musician or writer, but a child is sometimes better equipped than an adult to pass along tender mercies.

Father Robertson Paints the Walls

When she was growing up in 1860s rural New York, Anna Mary Robertson took her father's interest in art for granted. "When I was quite small my father would get me and my brothers white paper by the sheet," she recalls. "He liked to see us draw pictures, it was a penny a sheet and it lasted longer than candy." She colored her "pictures" with "grape juice or berries"—"the gayer the better."[3]

But her father did more than purchase paper. "Father was not well that winter, he had pneumonia." Heavy outside work went undone, but there was work inside the house that needed attention. He noticed how grimy the walls were. "One day he said to mother, 'Margaret, how would you like me to paint the walls?' And mother said she did not care, just so they were clean. So he commenced in one corner of the room and painted a scene that he had seen the spring before up at Lake George. It was so pretty, mother told him to do some more, so he painted different scenes all around the room."[4]

Times were hard, but the walls of the Robertson home brought smiles and cheered their spirits. Anna followed her father in painting memories—most often capturing ordinary days that might otherwise have been forgotten. As she reflected back, she realized that hardships and happiness often went hand in hand. The bitter cold of a winter day was easily brightened by playful children painted on a snowy landscape with colorful houses and barns. As Grandma Moses, she left a legacy of memories in her simple colorful paintings.

Prodded by what might be viewed as no more than a meager example set by her father and his routine encouragement of the children in their own artwork, Anna Mary, beginning at age seventy-five, went on to leave an incredible legacy. It is a legacy that has found its way into our home by way of a print of a winter scene that hangs on our family room wall. Her visual memories bring me back to my own childhood of farm life through the seasons. My favorite coffee table book, *Grandma Moses in the 21st Century*, features her lively "Moving Day on the Farm" on the cover, with page after page of colorful paintings inside.[5]

Daniel and Shamus

One of my favorite short stories is "Mothers' Day" by Octavus Roy Cohen.

It was Saturday night, the eve of Mothers' Day. Dan Clancy "neither knew nor cared." He was a police detective, "square-shouldered" and "erect," and "thought only of himself." But on this particular night his thoughts were on a "narrow-shouldered and furtive" drifter, "a sneak-thief" who was hiding under the freight cars a ways off.

Of course, Dan could have picked him up willy-nilly as a vagrant and seen to it that the man received thirty or sixty or

200

ninety days in the workhouse. But there was little pleasure in that. It amused Dan to play with his quarry as a cat plays with a mouse, when already the feline has partaken of a full meal. Perhaps desperation or hunger or the need of shelter for the frail body might drive the stranger to commit some petty offense. Time enough then to place the heavy hand of the law upon the narrow shoulders.

The detective stalked his prey until the derelict headed for the low-class business district and disappeared into a little store with a "shabby sign over the doorway" that read "Post-Card Exchange." Dan Clancy was puzzled as he peered through the outside window. Why would this drifter be browsing through the postcard racks, studying each one intently? It made no sense. But the dirty little man finally made his selection and dug into his pocket for a nickel to make the purchase. He then walked out the door and crossed the street to the telegraph office. There he made a transaction and disappeared into the night.

Dan Clancy let the worthless transient go, but his curiosity was piqued. He strolled across the street and into the office, showing his badge and demanding to know what the "little rat" was up to. The clerk reached into the drawer and pulled out the card, telling the detective that he had wired the message on a postcard and signed the drifter's name. The message read:

Mrs. Katie Clancy
819 Arcade Street
Portland
    To my Mother: My help and my inspiration,
    the one who has had faith in me always and who
    has stood by me in brightest day and darkest
    night. To my only sweetheart—My mother.
                    Your loving son—
                    Shamus

The detective stared at the card as he read it over and over. He gave it back to the clerk and started out the door, but then turned back. He walked over to the rack and reached for a blank telegram form and sat down at a table and began to write:

Mrs. Katie Clancy
819 Arcade Street
Portland
  Lots of love to the best Mother in the world
  on Mothers' Day. I saw Shamus today, and he is
  doing fine.
                              Your loving son—
                              Daniel[6]

Two brothers, Daniel and Shamus. But there is no mother in the story. We learn nothing about her except for a name and address. Was she a good mother whose heart had been broken: one son a failure, the other a success who cared nothing for her? Was she a negligent mother addicted to alcohol: one son escaping, the other following her down the path of indigence? We can only wonder. But it was a tender mercy from the son who had failed that made his brother realize that he too had failed.

As a mother, I still cherish a card that came from my then wayward son. Following the touching printed message is his scrawled handwriting: "Thanks for <u>everything</u> Mom. Sorry I'm not always the best but thanks for sticking with me. I love you tons." It was a card—a tender mercy—that buoyed my spirits as surely those postcards did for Katie Clancy.

A Cup of Cold Water and a Place to Die

Today we had an opportunity to pass on a tender mercy. In this case the cup of cold water was two pizzas. I was working outside when I greeted our next-door neighbor as she walked to her car. She came over to the fence to tell me that Michael from down the street had died suddenly of a heart attack three nights earlier and that today was his funeral. He was thirty-seven. She said that his wife, her good friend Jennie, and the two girls, would be staying with her family for the next several days. At that point Jennie herself walked over and we were introduced. I offered my condolences, but felt as they left for the funeral home that I wanted to do something more. So this evening we picked up pizzas and brought them to the neighbor's small house now crowded with three guests. This cup of cold water is hopefully only the first of many tender mercies that we will be privileged to pass on to Jennie in the months and years ahead.

Sometimes the cup of cold water is multiplied a thousand times a thousand, as in the case of Mother Teresa. One touch, one smile, one warm blanket all manifested in a way of life. The least of these for her were those who were dying—dying without loved ones, dying without a home. For Mother Teresa, such tender mercies came many times each day. For others, the privilege may come only once in a lifetime.

Mary was a farmer's wife.

Such a designation when I was growing up on a farm in northern Wisconsin was taken for granted. Jennie, my mother, was a farmer's wife. So also were Ruby and Ethel and Rachel and Freda and Tina. Most of these women I knew primarily for their good deeds. Part of their duties as farmers' wives was to keep a watchful eye on the neighborhood—to be there for the birth of a baby and the burial of the dearly departed. My mother was one of them. She was generous and quick to act in times of need. So was my father, but as the *farmer* his fieldwork came first.

"Mary sat musing on the lamp-flame at the table." This is the first line of Robert Frost's poem, "The Death of the Hired Man." She is waiting for her husband Warren to return home from the market. She meets him at the door to tell him the news: "Silas is back." Her next words are telling: "Be kind." But Warren had been kind to him. He responds adamantly: "I'll not have the fellow back." Silas was old and did not pull his weight. But that was not the critical issue for Warren. Silas had left him in the lurch: "Off he goes always when I need him most."

"Sh! . . . not so loud: he'll hear you. . . . He's worn out. He's asleep beside the stove. . . . Warren, he has come home to die: You needn't be afraid he'll leave you this time." Home? This is not home for Silas. He's a hired man, for heaven's sake—and an unreliable hired man at that. How could this be home? But then what is home?

"Home is the place where, when you have to go there,
    They have to take you in."[7]

Warren is not so easily convinced. If he's sick, he reasons, why can't he go live with his brother who has plenty of money to take care of him? Why does he have to come here? They talk on, remembering Silas's odd ways. Mary knows, as does her husband, that Silas was just trying to save face when he had told her he had come back "to help ditch the meadow" and "to clear the upper pasture, too." She urges Warren to go inside and talk to him.

Warren returned—too soon, it seemed to her,
    Slipped to her side, caught up her hand and waited.
    "Warren?" she questioned.
    "Dead," was all he answered.[8]

Mary was a farmer's wife. That's all we really know about her—except for the legacy of tender mercies she offered Silas in the fading moments of his life. Mary is no more than a fictional farmer's wife. Yet she rises above her farmer husband who was surely a good man. But Mary was more. Her legacy is forever secure—safe in the archives and annals of American poetry—reminding us of the profound opportunities we are offered for doing good even in the most ordinary circumstances of life.

18

FREE AT LAST

Epitaphs and Graveyard Reflections

As I'm sitting on the deck of our small getaway farmhouse in northern Michigan, I glance frequently from the computer screen and look out across the summer landscape. A Van Gogh patchwork of fields and forests stretches this way and that through the hillsides leading to the distant horizon. There is a depth of color and light and shadow that one rarely finds in the city or even on a body of water. The songs of birds and breezes are interrupted only occasionally by a passing car. There are no human voices—no laughter, no shouting, no singing. Yet as I glance over my shoulder I see a city—a city of the dead where the living talk in whispers and the dead only listen. In this remote setting, the stillness of the hillsides easily coexists with the serenity of the cemetery. Here new graves mingle with the old in this silent sepulchre where squeals of delight are only a memory.

I love to wander through cemeteries. I find solace there, and I find the past in stark reality. Here is raw history—not the history we find in the texts featuring great movers and shakers. Beneath the sod all are equal—rich and poor, scholars and simple folks. All that remains, apart from one's eternal destiny, is memory and legacy.

We ought to approach a cemetery with a "left-behind" mentality—not so much wondering about the state of the occupants' souls but rather contemplating what has been left behind. The Left Behind series, with all its popularity, is a distorted perspective on eschatology—and not just the particulars of the end times. Its singular focus on the rapture and what follows in the tribulation bypasses the legacy that is left behind here on earth. There is no room in this series for reflecting on the giant carbon footprint or the legacy of good deeds that the one ascending into heaven has left behind. It is a mentality that blatantly disregards future generations living here on earth.

When I Die

My husband and I talk often about death. I've heard many details about the months and weeks leading up to the passing of his two late wives, and he never tires of my asking questions. Their legacies live on even as their stories are remembered and retold. Neither one of them, however, opened up with him about their impending deaths. That's not my way. I would talk. We would have no-holds-barred conversations—if I have the advantage of forewarning. Nor will I go calmly and quietly. The lyrics of Dylan Thomas are mine: "Do not go gentle into that good night. . . . Rage, rage against the dying of the light."

The matters of legacy and death are closely related. We all know that our days are numbered. Yet we are tempted to imagine we're invincible. We are shocked to learn of a friend's untimely accidental death or of a diagnosis of terminal cancer. Death and the finality of the legacy that follows easily seem far away unless we have the heads-up of a terminal diagnosis. How different life would be if our death date were not so uncertain. What if humans were programmed, like the cicada, to have a very precise life span?

We're most familiar with those that emerge from the ground after developing in nymph stage for seventeen years. They mate, and then in a few weeks, right on schedule, they die. Imagine our human life span paralleling that of this insect—of growing up fully aware of a set life span. How would we live life differently? Would such knowledge affect our decision making? Would the matter of legacy be more prominent on our radar screens?

I easily imagine myself living another thirty or forty years with plenty of time to get my house—and my legacy—in order. After all, I'm young. I'm still in my early sixties. I eat well and exercise and schedule regular medical checkups—and I have longevity in my genes. Apart from the accidental death of my mother, my elders have all lived on into their late seventies and eighties and beyond. But this morning I was surprised to learn that I may not have as many years left as I had hoped. "The Death Clock" at www.deathclock.com doesn't even get me into my eighties. The medical specialists with the calculations have set my death at September 28, 2024 (giving me a grand total of 530,640,151 seconds before I expire). Husband John will be checking out on April 24, 2014, barely six years away. He will not celebrate his seventy-fourth birthday. That, despite the fact that he can hop on his bike and ride some fifty miles (to Sand Lake and back) and then work in the yard the rest of the afternoon. That, despite the fact that his father lived on into his eighties (with a serious heart condition) and that his mother at ninety-three is living independently and in good health. So much for the death clock.

But are we really prepared to die? That question is most frequently asked in reference to our eternal state. As such it is surely a valid question. But there is another side of the coin. On the one side is the bliss of eternal life, on the other side is the sum of a legacy left behind with no opportunity to add to what is left undone.

A Deathbed Stream of Consciousness

Caught in a rush of a Colorado raging river. To hear Darlene and Kathy tell it, interrupting each other and clipping their words, you would think it happened yesterday. There's something compelling about those life-and-death stories of sheer terror and inexplicable survival. Some testify, *My life flashed before me.* How does a life flash in a matter of seconds or minutes? I do not know apart from the stories of others. One of the most mesmerizing torrent of memories that I know comes from the pen of Katherine Anne Porter. The short story is entitled "The Jilting of Granny Weatherall."

Granny is eighty, in bed, and experiencing a relatively peaceful death. Her life meanders "while she is rummaging around in her mind." She senses she is dying and she has a few regrets about things undone: "All those letters—George's letters and John's letters and her letters to them both—lying around for the children to find afterwards made her uneasy. Yes that would be tomorrow's business. No use to let them know how silly she had been once." She reflects on times gone by—on the legacy she is leaving behind:

> In her day she had kept a better house and had got more work done. They had been so sweet when they were little, Granny wished the old days were back again with the children young and everything to be done over. It had been a hard pull, but not too much for her. When she thought of all the food she had cooked and all the clothes she had cut and sewed, and all the gardens she had made—well the children showed it. There they were made out of her, and they couldn't get away from that. Sometimes she wanted to see John again and point to them and say, Well, I didn't do so badly, did I? But that would have to wait. . . . She had fenced in a hundred acres once, digging the post holes herself and clamping the wires with just a negro boy to help. That changed a woman. . . . Digging post holes changed a woman. Riding country roads in the winter when women had their babies was another thing. . . . John, I hardly ever lost one of them.[1]

But as the word *jilting* in the title suggests, Granny's stream of consciousness also picks up on another theme. Amid the hard times—including daughter Hapsy's death—that still-raw anguishing moment of betrayal continues to haunt her. She cannot get away from the man who left her standing at the altar. Looking back, she has no regrets that she did not marry him. John was a good husband, and he gave her beloved children and grandchildren. No regrets. *All things work together for good.* Yet the sting of betrayal never dies. One legacy and another blended like cake batter. Raw eggs and flour and sugar. In the end the cake is done and Granny's life work is but a legacy.

Laws, Immigration, and Legacy

I enjoy reading eulogies or epitaphs that I find inserted in a book or essay—often inserted for their power in arguing an otherwise unrelated matter. Paul Greenberg wrote his July 4, 2007, syndicated editorial on his disappointment over the death of the Immigration Bill in Congress—arguing that, with all its problems, it was better than no immigration bill at all. One of those problems took a personal slant as the dead legislation intersected with memories of his deceased mother:

> We're all products of our own experience, and the first thing I thought when reading an outline of this voluminous monstrosity was: Ma would never have made the cut.
>
> Yes, my mother was young and strong. But she had not formal schooling, not at all. She was, as we like to say in the family, illiterate in five languages. That's what growing up on a battlefield of the First World War, Eastern Front, will give you: a true European education. Her major was suffering.
>
> What she wanted most in life, desperately wanted, and would have overcome all obstacles to achieve, and just did, was to be . . . an American. She wanted work, safety, respect, a home, a family, a chance.

But that chance would have been denied her by this bill because, if passed, it would have operated on the point system— "points for English proficiency, experience living here, a solid job offer" and many more things Greenberg's mother did not possess.[2] Her desperate desire to raise a family in America parallels the longings of my own ancestors. They also would have scored low

209

by today's immigration standards. For Greenberg's mother, the lack of points would have prevented her from leaving an ordinary American family legacy as she did—one passed on by her son as an epitaph to her life.

Fitting and Unfitting Epitaphs

What words would I have inscribed on my tombstone? I imagine that, like John's two dearly departed wives, I will have a simple stone with name and dates. But if I were to sum up my legacy in fifty words or less, what would I write—or what would others write? As I look back in history, I discover as many false epitaphs as true. Many individuals who were well-known and highly regarded in their day have lost their luster through the passage of time. It is interesting to compare the epitaphs of Alexander Hamilton and Thomas Jefferson, both founding fathers but bitter political enemies. Today Jefferson is the one whom schoolchildren remember. Hamilton is more likely forgotten, though his epitaph (written by others) would suggest otherwise:

ALEXANDER HAMILTON
TRINITY CHURCHYARD,
NEW YORK, NEW YORK
IN TESTIMONY OF THEIR RESPECT
FOR
THE PATRIOT OF INCORRUPTIBLE INTEGRITY,
THE SOLDIER OF APPROVED VALOUR
THE STATESMAN OF CONSUMMATE WISDOM;
WHOSE TALENTS AND VIRTUES WILL BE ADMIRED
BY
GRATEFUL POSTERITY
LONG AFTER THIS MARBLE SHALL HAVE MOULDERED INTO DUST

Jefferson wrote his own inscription—words that almost seem to diminish his legacy. His rationale was true to his concept of legacy, however. Although he served as vice president (under John Adams) and president for two terms, he insisted that he wanted to be remembered for what he gave to America, and not what America had given to him. Thus his epitaph was spare:

THOMAS JEFFERSON
MONTICELLO, VIRGINIA
AUTHOR OF THE DECLARATION OF AMERICAN INDEPENDENCE
OF THE STATUTE OF VIRGINIA FOR RELIGIOUS FREEDOM
AND FATHER OF THE UNIVERSITY OF VIRGINIA.

Decades after the founding fathers died another founding father died—the founding father of the Confederate States of America. His epitaph seems to imply that he was an ordinary soldier and government official. It gives no indication that he played such a significant role during the Civil War as the president of the Confederacy.

JEFFERSON DAVIS
AT REST
AN AMERICAN SOLDIER
AND DEFENDER OF THE CONSTITUTION
(1808–1889)

The very simple lyrics of an oft-quoted old Negro spiritual serve as a most fitting epitaph for a man whose legacy needs no further explanation:

MARTIN LUTHER KING, JR.
FREE AT LAST, FREE AT LAST. THANK GOD ALMIGHTY
WE ARE FREE AT LAST.

Susanna Wesley's Epitaph

One of the most misleading epitaphs I have ever encountered in my studies is the one written by Charles Wesley for his mother Susanna Wesley. Charles is the lesser known of the Wesley brothers—except among church musicians. John is considered the founder of the Methodist church. Charles was the much-heralded hymn writer whose lyrics are sung in every denomination and around the world today. And the Christmas season does not seem complete without his "Hark! the Herald Angels Sing."

When Mother Wesley died in the summer of 1742, at age seventy-two, she was buried at Bunhill Fields. Son John preached the funeral sermon and son Charles served as poet, penning the lines for her epitaph. The first stanza that speaks of her crown and mansion in the skies appears to be no more than a son's sentimentality. But suddenly in the second stanza, the sentimentality veers into a serious allegation—that her life consisted of "a legal night of seventy years." The third stanza catches her in free fall, when the Father revealed his Son and she felt her sins forgiven:

> In sure and steadfast hope to rise,
> And claim her mansion in the skies,
> A Christian here her flesh laid down,
> The cross exchanging for a crown.
>
> True daughter of affliction, she,
> Inured to pain and misery,
> Mourn'd a long night of griefs and fears,
> A legal night of seventy years.
>
> The Father then revealed his Son;
> Him in the broken bread made known;
> She knew and felt her sins forgiven,
> And found the earnest of her heaven.
>
> Meet for the fellowship above,
> She heard the call, "Arise, my love!"
> "I come!" her dying looks replied,
> And, lamb-like as her Lord, she died.

Having studied and written about the life of Susanna Wesley, I find this poem of Charles more than just insulting. With these words (apparently approved by his brother), he sought to erase the extraordinary legacy of his mother. Fortunately, his assessment is today forgotten, and his epitaph is now but a footnote summed up by a nineteenth-century Wesley biographer who says it best:

When she died in 1742, her sons had four verses inscribed on her tombstone, teaching, if they teach anything, that she was not received into the divine favor until she attained the age of seventy. This is a monstrous perversion of facts, and can only be accounted for on the ground that John and Charles Wesley were so enamored of their blessed and newly discovered doctrines, that as yet they felt it difficult to think any one to be scripturally converted except those who . . . had experienced an instantaneous change of heart, under circumstances similar to their own. . . . Having read her letters and her other literary productions, we are satisfied that, if there ever was a sincere and earnest Christian, she was one.[3]

Susanna's legacy has long been dear to my heart—so much so that John and I drove out of our way to visit the Wesley home. We spent a sunny September afternoon meandering through her house and gardens in Epworth, England. As ministers' wives and as mothers, Susanna and I have commonality—though as children go, she trumps me nineteen to one. I can't imagine how she managed to conduct an organized household and even do a little preaching on the side (when her husband was away). But most of all, I find in her a model of a feisty woman—strong, independent, and opinionated. She stood up to her husband when he tried to silence her, holding fast to her "little liberty of conscience."

Despite their slighting of their mother's legacy, I have great respect for the Wesley brothers. John especially was a humble man who questioned his own worthiness throughout his life. Biographers have suggested that he may have gone to the grave without assurance of salvation. In the winter of 1753 when he thought he was dying, he wrote his own epitaph:

HERE LIETH THE BODY

OF

JOHN WESLEY,

A BRAND PLUCKED OUT OF THE BURNING:

WHO DIED OF A CONSUMPTION IN THE FIFTY-FIRST YEAR OF HIS AGE,

NOT LEAVING, AFTER HIS DEBTS ARE PAID,

TEN POUNDS BEHIND HIM:

PRAYING

GOD BE MERCIFUL, TO ME, AN UNPROFITABLE SERVANT!

John did not die at fifty. He lived on for more than thirty-seven years to 1791. Though he saw himself as an unprofitable servant, he surely must have heard the same words that had welcomed his mother and his younger brother:

Well done, good and faithful servant.

Epilogue

As I stand on my soapbox for a few final paragraphs, I would challenge the reader to contemplate one last time leadership and legacy.

For those of you who consider yourselves leaders, stand up, take out a pen and pad, and jot down the names of your actual followers—not counting family members and those paid as employees to *follow* you. Sit down if your list is no more than one. If you're a guide or a conductor or a military sergeant or a cult prophet or leadership guru, sit down. For those still standing with two followers or more, jot down a list of the books and seminars and other leadership programs that transformed you into a leader. If your list mirrors even a small education of at least a half-dozen seminars, contact me through my publisher for a prize.

Leadership is as fuzzy as it is shady and slippery—fuzzy in that it is so universally used without comprehension, and shady and slippery because bad so easily masks as good and often cancels out good. Indeed, the damage left in the wake of bad leaders in the history of the world far exceeds the benefits bestowed by good leaders. And it's safe to say that the good leaders we remember have no connection with the contemporary fad promoted by the leadership industry.

Legacy, on the other hand, is much more accessible and more easily understood. It is for everyone. All of us one day will have our legacy judged. The biblical story from Daniel 5 comes to mind. King Belshazzar is having a grand banquet, and all of a sudden, he sees the fingers of a human hand writing on the plaster wall. None of his diviners can interpret the meaning, so Daniel is brought forth. He sees the writing on the wall. His interpretation sums up Belshazzar's legacy. It is blunt: *Thou art weighed in the balances and art found wanting.*

As we contemplate our legacy footprint, we must honestly assess our lives. What are we living for and what will we leave behind for generations that follow? As with our carbon footprint, the good is mixed with the bad.

Dietrich Bonhoeffer challenges us to look deep into our own souls. His legacy is profound. A Lutheran cleric in Nazi Germany, he fought the powers of evil and stood for what was right. He languished in prison before he was executed. His prison letters to his beloved Maria and to others show an ordinary man in many ways—surely not the super saint we have fashioned. His very personal reflections in his poem "Who Am I?" challenge us all to assess our motives and actions as we contemplate our legacy and our place in this world. He looked back over his life and wondered if he deserved the accolades others accorded him, or if he were actually no more than a hypocrite—"a woebegone weakling." Who am I? He repeats the haunting question and then offers his self-identity as his final legacy: "Whoever I am, Thou knowest, O God, I am thine!"

NOTES

Introduction

1. Richard Stengel, "Choosing Order Before Freedom," *Time,* December 31, 2007, 45.

2. Adi Ignatius, "A Tsar Is Born," *Time,* December 31, 2007, 48; "The Time Interview: Putin Opens the Window on His Life," ibid., 51.

3. Ignatius, "A Tsar Is Born," 46.

4. Jonathan Steele, "Putin's Legacy Is a Russia That Doesn't Have to Curry Favour with the West," *Guardian,* September 18, 2007, 2.

Chapter 1 Leadership 620

1. Parker Palmer, *The Courage to Teach: Exploring the Inner Landscape of a Teacher's Life* (San Francisco: Jossey-Bass, 1998), 85–86, 101.

2. Cited in ibid., 28.

3. Ibid., 2.

4. James MacGregor Burns, *Leadership* (New York: HarperCollins, 1978), 2.

5. Kenneth Blanchard in Leadership Inspirational Quotes & Insights for Leaders, http://www.uca.edu/divisions/Student/leadership/leadershipdevelopment.htm.

6. Ronald A. Heifetz and Marty Linsky, *Leadership on the Line: Staying Alive through the Dangers of Leading* (Boston: Harvard Business School Press, 2002), 1.

7. John J. Sullivan, *Servant First! Leadership for the New Millennium* (n.p.: Xulon, 2003), 99.

8. Richard H. G. Field, "Leadership Defined: Web Images Reveal the Differences between Leadership and Management," January 9, 2002, http://www.business.ualberta.ca/rfield/papers/LeadershipDefined.htm.

9. Warren Bennis, "Sayings and Quotes," http://www.sayings-quotes.com/warren_bennis_quotes/.

10. Ronald A. Heifetz, *Leadership without Easy Answers* (Cambridge: Harvard University, 1994), 16.

11. Ibid.

12. Ibid., 17.

13. Ibid., 16–17.

14. Ibid., 20.

15. Carter McNamara, "Leadership Cube (TM) to Contextualize Leadership," 1997–2007, http://www.managementhelp.org/ldrship/carters.htm.

16. Ibid.

17. Jill Lepore, "Noah's Mark: Webster and the Original Dictionary Wars," *New Yorker*, November 6, 2006, 78.

18. Ibid., 82.

19. Ibid., 86.

Chapter 2 PowerPoint Presentations

1. http://www.crcna.org/pages/sesqui_institute.cfm.

2. Rachel Gordon, "Willie Brown Comes Home to Roost at S.F. State," *San Francisco Chronicle,* November 8, 2007, B3.

3. Ibid.

4. Richard Barker, "How Can We Train Leaders If We Do Not Know What Leadership Is?" *Human Relations,* April 1997, 343–62, http://www.springerlink.com/content/g5m305866517385x/.

5. Michael Kinsley, "Bring in the Consultants!" *Time*, November 26, 2007, 27.

6. Ibid.

7. Jay Conger, "Can We Really Train Leadership?" http://www.strategy-business.com/press/16635507/8714.

8. Bruce Byfield, "Business Experts and the Cult of Leadership," Off the Wall: Bruce Byfield's Blog, June 22, 2007, http://brucebyfield.wordpress.com/2007/06/22/business-experts-and-the-cult-of-leadership/.

9. Susan Heathfield's "Secrets of Leadership Success," http://humanresources.about.com/od/leadership/a/leader_success.htm.

10. Don Clark, "About Big Dog and Little Dog's Bowl of Biscuits," accessed October 29, 2007, http://www.nwlink.com/~Donclark/about/about.html.

11. Ibid.

12. Don Clark, "Leading and Leadership," http://www.nwlink.com/~Donclark/leader/leadled.html.

13. Byfield, "Business Experts," June 22, 2007, http://brucebyfield.wordpress.com/2007/06/22/business-experts-and-the-cult-of-leadership/.

14. "Leadership Training for the Real World," Leadership IQ, http://www.leadershipiq.com/.

15. Leadership IQ, http://www.leadershipiq.com/.

16. Ibid.

17. "Essential Skills for Your Excellent Career!" Mind Tools, www.mindtools.com.

18. Ibid.

Chapter 3 The Ladder of Success

1. Warren Meyer, "In Praise of 'Robber Barons,'" Coyote Blog, http://www.coyote
blog.com/coyote_blog/2005/02/in_praise_of_ro.html.

2. Janet C. Lowe, *Warren Buffett Speaks: Wit and Wisdom from the World's Greatest Investor* (New York: John Wiley & Sons, 1997), 165–66.

3. Bill George, "The Master Gives It Back," *US News & World Report*, October 22, 2006, 3, http://www.usnews.com/usnews/news/articles/061022/30buffett_3.htm.

4. Lowe, *Warren Buffett Speaks*, 164–65.

5. Larry Kanter, "Brilliant Careers: Warren Buffet," *Salon*, August 31, 1999, 1, http://www.salon.com/people/bc/1999/08/31/buffett/index1.html.

6. Parker Palmer, *The Courage to Teach: Exploring the Inner Landscape of a Teacher's Life* (San Francisco: Jossey-Bass, 1998), 101.

Chapter 4 Hitler and Thomas the Tank

1. David Wilcock, "The Rev. Wilbert Awdry . . . Dies at 85," http://www.pegnsean.net/~railwayseries/awdryobit.htm.

2. Wilbert Vere Awdry, "Thomas's Only Begetter," http://www.awdry.family.name/wilbert-awdry.htm.

3. Ibid.

4. Mack Teasley interview with Kurt Heilbronn, March 9, 1993, http://www.ibiblio.org/lia/president/EisenhowerLibrary/oral_histories/Heilbronn_Kurt.html.

5. Rudolf Hess, "Electing Adolf Hitler Führer," German Propaganda Archive, Calvin College, http://www.calvin.edu/academic/cas/gpa/hess2.htm.

6. "Rudolf Hess," The History Place, 1996, http://www.historyplace.com/worldwar2/biographies/hess-bio.htm.

7. Ronald A. Heifetz, *Leadership without Easy Answers* (Cambridge: Harvard University, 1994), 24.

8. Dale Van Atta, "World's Most Dangerous Leaders," *Reader's Digest,* July 2007, 139–42.

9. Barbara Kellerman, *Bad Leadership: What It Is, How It Happens, Why It Matters* (Boston: Harvard Business School Press, 2004), 11.

10. Ibid., 5.

11. Barbara Kellerman interviewed by Molly Lanzarotta, May 3, 2005, http://www.ksg.harvard.edu/ksgnews/KSGInsight/kellerman.htm.

12. Cited in Gordon Trowbridge, "Iacocca Bashes Bush in New Book: Ex-Chrysler CEO Also Rips Congress, but the Harshest Criticism Goes to President's Leadership," *Detroit News*, April 12, 2007, http://www.detnews.com/apps/pbcs.dll/article?AID=/20070412/POLITICS/704120383.

13. Heifetz, *Leadership without Easy Answers*, 13, 14.

14. Ibid., 14.

15. David Leonhardt, "Thomas the Tank Story Can Teach Us a Lesson," *Grand Rapids Press*, June 24, 2007, G3.

16. Ibid.

Chapter 5 God's CEO

1. Don Blohowiak, "Thou Shalt Heed and Honor Ancient Lessons," Lead Well Institute, http://www.leadwell.com/db/1/4/232/.
2. "Faculty Spotlight: Dr. Sid Buzzell," Colorado Christian University, http://www.ccu.edu/admissions/spotlight/spotlight.asp?iSpotID=239.
3. Sid Buzzell, gen. ed., *The Leadership Bible: Leadership Principles from God's Word* (Grand Rapids: Zondervan, 1998), ix.
4. http://www.faithandworkresources.com/store_items_view.asp?itemid=15734.
5. *The Leadership Bible*, 7.
6. Ibid., 3.
7. Ibid., 1113.
8. Ibid., 73.
9. *The Bible on Leadership*, http://www.amanet.org/books/catalog/0814406823.htm.
10. Ibid., 1391.
11. Martin Luther cited in Mark Shaw, *10 Great Ideas from Church History* (Downers Grove, IL: InterVarsity, 1997), 35.
12. Donald A. Carson, *From Triumphalism to Maturity: An Exposition of 2 Corinthians 10–13* (Grand Rapids: Baker, 1984), 117.
13. Dick Tripp, "The Function of Leadership," Exploring Christianity: The Church, http://www.christianity.co.nz/church7.htm; (original emphasis).
14. Ibid.
15. Ibid.
16. Gordon MacDonald, "The Root of Leadership," *Leadership*, Winter 2003, 55–56.
17. Ibid., 58.

Chapter 6 Jesus as Model

1. John Paul II, Beatification of Mother Teresa of Calcutta, http://www.vatican.va/holy_father/john_paul_ii/homilies/2003/documents/hf_jp-ii_hom_2003 1019_mother-theresa_en.html.
2. http://en.wikipedia.org/wiki/Servant_leadership.
3. Ibid.
4. Ibid.
5. Matthew Waller, "A New View of Leadership," *Baylor Magazine*, Spring 2007, 33; "Q&A: Servant Leadership with Frank Shuskok," http://www.baylormag.com/story.php?story=006036.
6. R. K. Greenleaf, *Servant Leadership: A Journey into the Nature of Legitimate Power and Greatness*, 25th anniversary ed. (New York: Paulist, 2002), 27.
7. "Fire Destroys Malden Mills," Mass Moments, http://www.massmoments.org/moment.cfm?mid=355.
8. Ibid.
9. Tom Jablonski, "Who Is a Servant Leader?" Servant-Leadership Blog, http://servantleadershipblog.com/servant-leadership/blog/2006/09/who-is-servant-leader.html.

10. John Woolman, *Journal of John Woolman*, 178, Electronic Text Center, University of Virginia Library, http://etext.lib.virginia.edu/etcbin/toccer-new2?id=WooJour .sgm&images=images/modeng&data=/texts/english/modeng/parsed&tag=public& part=1&division=div1.

11. Ibid., 185.

12. Ibid., 186.

13. Robert Greenleaf, *Servant Leadership: A Journey into the Nature of Legitimate Power and Greatness* (New York: Paulist, 1977), 43.

14. Ibid.

Chapter 7 Martin Luther King Jr.

1. David L. Cawthon, "Leadership: The Great Man Theory Revisited," *Business Horizons*, May–June 1996, 1–3.

2. Warren Bennis and Burt Nanus, cited in ibid.

3. Ian Chamberlain, Winston Churchill Leadership, http://www.winston-churchill-leadership.com/index.html.

4. Thomas Wagner, "Papers Show Churchill's Cabinet Battles," AP News, *Grand Rapids Press*, November 1, 2007, A4.

5. Ibid.

6. Heifetz, *Leadership without Easy Answers*, 16.

7. Ibid., 207.

8. Ibid., 20.

9. Ibid., 219.

10. Ibid., 222.

11. Richard Lischer, *The Preacher King: Martin Luther King, Jr. and the Word That Moved America* (New York: Oxford University Press, 1995), 23–24.

12. Ibid., 24.

13. Ibid.

14. Garry Wills, *Certain Trumpets: The Nature of Leadership* (New York: Simon & Schuster, 1994), 215–16.

15. Ibid., 218.

16. Cited in ibid., 219.

17. Cited in Philip Yancey, *Soul Survivor: How My Faith Survived the Church* (New York: Doubleday, 2001), 13, 20–21.

18. Ibid., 12–15.

19. Ibid., 19.

Chapter 8 Personality and Power

1. Cited in Terry Macalister, "Fallen Titans Show Charisma Is the Most Volatile Stock of All," *Guardian*, October 9, 2007, http://www.guardian.co.uk/business/2007/ oct/09/5.

2. Ibid.

3. Trowbridge, "Iacocca Bashes Bush," http://www.detnews.com/apps/pbcs.dll/ article?AID=/20070412/POLITICS/704120383.

4. Eli Harari, The Thinking Coach, http://www.thethinkingcoach.com/meet_eli.htm.

5. Stephen R. Covey, *The 7 Habits of Highly Effective People* (New York: Simon & Schuster, 1989), 18.

6. Ibid., 19.

7. "The Personality and the President Project," Testing the Presidents, http://www.testingthepresidents.com/.

8. Steven J. Rubenzer and Thomas R. Faschingbauer, *Personality, Character, and Leadership in the White House* (Washington, DC: Potomac Books, 2004), 7.

9. Ibid., 7–11.

10. Ibid., 15, 19, 43.

11. Ibid., 23, 43.

12. Ibid., 50.

13. Ibid., 31.

14. Cited in Dale Carnegie, *Lincoln the Unknown* (Garden City, NY: Dale Carnegie Associates, 1959), 119.

15. Donald T. Phillips, *Lincoln on Leadership: Executive Strategies for Tough Times* (New York: Warner Books, 1992), 26, 37, 98.

Chapter 9 Girl Scouts and More

1. "Intelligence Report," *Parade*, December 16, 2007, 10.

2. Emil Brunner, *Man in Revolt* (New York, 1939), 358–59.

3. Sojourner Truth, "Ain't I a Woman?" December 1851, *Modern History Sourcebook*, http://www.fordham.edu/halsall/mod/sojtruth-woman.html.

4. Covey, *7 Habits*, 147.

5. Ibid., 130.

6. Ruth H. Howes and Michael Stevenson, eds., *Women and the Use of Military Force* (Boulder, CO: Lynne Reinner, 1993), 212.

7. Jim Collison, "Female Bosses Rate Higher as Effective Leaders: What Must Employers and Males Do?" http://www.employerhelp.org/jimcollison/stories/female_bosses.htm.

8. Maria Bartiromo, "Head of the Troops," *Reader's Digest,* August 2007, 69.

9. Ibid., 70.

10. Ibid., 69.

11. Lev Grossman, "The Doubting Harry," *Time,* July 23, 2007, 15.

Chapter 10 Where Have All the Followers Gone?

1. Peter Drucker, "Thought on Leadership," *Leading Questions,* http://edbrenegar.typepad.com/leading_questions/2005/12/thoughts_on_lea.html.

2. Malcolm Forbes, "3 Principles That Define Leadership," *Strategic Junior High,* http://www.strategicjuniorhigh.com/ministry/3-principles-that-define-leadership/.

3. Tom Atchison, *Followership: A Practical Guide to Aligning Leaders and Followers* (Ann Arbor, MI: Health Administration Press, 2003), 43.

4. Warren Bennis and Burt Nanus, *Leaders* (New York: HarperCollins, 1986), 32.

5. John Maxwell, *Leadership 101*, http://www.amazon.com/gp/reader/0785264191/ref=sib_dp_pt#reader-link.

6. Ira Chaleff, "Courageous Followers, Courageous Leaders: New Relationships for Learning and Performance," Executive Coaching & Consulting Associates, December 2001, http://www.exe-coach.com/courageous.htm.

7. George R. Goethais et al., eds., *Encyclopedia of Leadership* (Thousand Oaks, CA: Sage Publications, 2004), 504.

8. Ibid., 505.

9. Garry Wills, *Certain Trumpets: The Nature of Leadership* (New York: Simon & Schuster, 1994), 11–12.

10. Ibid., 11–13.

11. Warren Bennis, "Followership," *USC Business*, Summer 1994, http://www.graphicarts.org/nalc/articles/follower.htm.

12. Kenneth Westhues, *The Envy of Excellence: Administrative Mobbing of High-Achieving Professors* (Lewiston, NY: Edwin Mellen, 2004, 2006), 29.

13. Brian Martin, "The Richardson Dismissal as an Academic Boomerang," in *Workplace Mobbing in Academe*, ed. Kenneth Westhues (Queenston, ON: Edwin Mellen, 2004), http://www.uow.edu.au/arts/sts/bmartin/pubs/04Westhues.html.

14. "Ask Jeanne Marie Laskas," *Reader's Digest*, January 2008, 71.

15. Eugene Peterson, "The Jonah Syndrome," *Leadership*, Summer 1990, 40.

16. Ruth A. Tucker, *Another Gospel: Alternative Religions and the New Age Movement* (Grand Rapids: Zondervan, 1989), 367–68.

17. Cited in ibid., 368.

18. Mark MacNamara, "The Return of Werner Erhard: Guru II," *Los Angeles Magazine*, May 1988, 106.

19. Ibid.

Chapter 11 President of the Internet

1. From "Herman Trend Alert," by Roger Herman and Joyce Gioia, in "Words to Lead By," Lead Well, http://www.leadwell.com/db/1/17/.

2. Kellerman, *Bad Leadership*, xv.

3. Kinsley, "Bring in the Consultants!" 27.

4. Margaret J. Wheatley, *Leadership and the New Science: Discovering Order in a Chaotic World*, 3rd ed. (San Francisco: Berrett-Koehler, 2006), 4.

5. Ibid., 7–8.

6. Ibid., 173, 175.

7. Peter Miller, "Swarm Theory," *National Geographic*, July 2007, 130–32.

8. Robert D. Steele, "Review: Compelling and Sensible, Offers Hope in Face of High-Level Threats," January 23, 2007, http://www.amazon.com/Starfish-Spider-Unstoppable-Leaderless-Organizations/dp/1591841437/ref=pd_bbs _sr_1/105-6627229-1376444?ie=UTF8&s=books&qid=1185927949&sr=8-1.

9. David Gergen, "America's Best Leaders," *U.S. News & World Report*, October 30, 2006, 39.

Chapter 12 Legacy 620

1. Jean Bethke Elshtain, *Jane Addams and the Dream of American Democracy: A Life* (New York: Basic Books, 2002), 119–21.

2. Jerry Apps, *Every Farm Tells a Story: A Tale of Family Farm Values* (Stillwater, MN: Voyageur, 2005), 148.

3. Sarah McIntyre, email, July 1, 2007.

4. Francesco Marcuilano, "Sally Forth," *Grand Rapids Press*, June 25, 2007, D2.

5. Samuel Johnson, *Adventurer and Idler*, in *The Works of Samuel Johnson, LL.D.*, vol. 4, no. 23, Saturday, September 23, 1758 (London: William Pickering, 1725), 216–17.

6. Ibid.

7. Ruth A. Tucker, *Women in the Maze: Questions and Answers on Biblical Equality* (Downers Grove, IL: InterVarsity, 1992), 9.

8. Ibid.

Chapter 13 Jefferson and Jefferson

1. Ernest J. Gaines, *A Lesson Before Dying* (New York: Random House, 1993), 223–24.

2. Ibid., 227.

3. Biography of Ernest J. Gaines, University of Louisiana at Lafayette, http://www.louisiana.edu/Academic/LiberalArts/ENGL/Creative/Gaines.htm.

4. Thomas Jefferson, *Notes on Virginia*, comp. Henry Augustine Washington (n.p.: Taylor & Maury, 1954), 403.

5. "Oprah Winfrey Debuts as First African-American on Business Week's Annual Ranking of 'America's Top Philanthropists,'" November 19, 2004, http://www.urbanmecca.com/artman/publish/article_174.shtml.

6. "Special Report—Philanthropy: African American Giving Comes of Age," *Business Week*, November 29, 2004, http://www.businessweek.com/magazine/content/04_48/b3910417.htm.

7. Ibid., 241.

Chapter 14 The Lemon Factor

1. Barbara Sapinsley, *The Private War of Mrs. Packard* (New York: Kodansha, 1995), 66.

2. Ibid., 69.

3. Ibid., 63.

4. Ibid., 73.

5. Ibid., xii.

6. Ibid., 79, 97, 138–39.

7. Ibid., 7.

8. Ibid., 227.

9. David Fellerath, "The Trials of Darryl Hunt: North Carolina Justice on Film Again," *Independent Weekly*, February 15, 2006, http://www.indyweek.com/gyrobase/Content?oid=oid%3A27818.

10. Ibid.

11. Kenneth Miller, "Missing: When People Disappear, Monica Caison Gets the Call," *Reader's Digest*, July 2007, 165.

12. Ibid., 167.

13. Ibid., 174.

14. Ibid.

15. Victor E. Frankl, *Man's Search for Meaning* (New York: Simon & Schuster, 1963), 122.

16. Anna Redsand, *Viktor Frankl: A Life Worth Living* (New York: Clarion Books, 2006), 26, 28, 29.

17. Ibid., 33.

18. Frankl, *Man's Search*, 12.

Chapter 15 An Earthkeeping Legacy

1. Rob Moll, "The Good Shepherds," *Christianity Today*, October 2007, 66.

2. "Energy and Emissions, Calvin and Carbon," *Calvin News* V3 #3378, November 27, 2007; "What Would It Take to Make Calvin a Carbon Neutral Campus?" November 29, 2007.

3. Tara Church, "Where the Leaders Are: The Promise of Youth Leadership," in *The Future of Leadership*, ed. Warren Bennis et al. (San Francisco: Jossey-Bass, 2001), 213–14.

4. Ibid., 305.

5. "To the Woodshed," *Parade*, July 8, 2007, 10.

6. Press editorial, "Time to Trash Wasteful Habits," *Grand Rapids Press*, July 3, 2007, A8.

7. M. R. Kropko, "Youngstown Copes by Thinking Small," Associated Press, *Grand Rapids Press*, June 25, 2007, B6.

8. Ibid.

9. Jane Lampman, "Churches Go Green," *Christian Science Monitor*, January 23, 2003, http://www.csmonitor.com/2003/0123/p11s02–lire.html.

10. *Grand Rapids Press*, June 17, 2007, A3.

11. Kathi Appelt, *Miss Lady Bird's Wildflowers: How a First Lady Changed America* (San Francisco: HarperCollins, 2005), 35.

12. Ibid., 36–37.

Chapter 16 Smile When I'm Gone

1. Ruth Tucker, *Left Behind in a Megachurch World: How God Works Through Ordinary Churches* (Grand Rapids: Baker, 2006), 144.

2. Dan Ferber, "The Funny Factor: Why Smart Brains Take Humor Seriously," *Reader's Digest*, September 2006, 102, 104–5.

3. Ibid., 103.

4. Constance Rourke, "The Comic Poet," *American Humor*, chap. V, http://xroads .virginia.edu/~hyper/rourke/ch05.html.

5. Mark Twain, Letter from Carson City, *Territorial Enterprise*, December 5, 1863, http://www.twainquotes.com/18631205t.html.

6. Gordon MacDonald, "Lake Wobegon's Prodigal Son," *Christianity Today*, May 18, 1992, 33.

7. Ibid.

8. Ibid.

9. Garrison Keillor, *Lake Wobegon Summer of 1956* (New York: Viking, 2001), 20.

10. Ruth A. Tucker, *Seasons of Motherhood: A Garden of Memories* (Wheaton: Victor, 1996), 243.

Chapter 17 Tender Mercies

1. Marilynne Robinson, *Gilead* (New York: Farrar, Straus, and Giroux, 2004), 51–52.

2. C. S. Lewis, *Surprised by Joy* (New York: Harvest, 1966), 14.

3. Anna Mary Robertson Moses, *My Life's History* (New York: HarperCollins, 1952), 26ff.

4. Ibid.

5. Jane Kallir, *Grandma Moses in the 21st Century* (New Haven: Yale University Press, 2001).

6. Octavus Roy Cohen, "Mothers' Day," in *The Mothers' Anthology*, comp. William Lyon Phelps (New York: Doubleday, Doran & Co., 1940), 100–110.

7. Robert Frost, "The Death of the Hired Man," 1915, in *Great Books Online*, http://www.bartleby.com/118/3.html.

8. Ibid.

Chapter 18 Free at Last

1. Katherine Anne Porter, "The Jilting of Granny Weatherall," in Bruce Weber, ed., *Look Who's Talking: An Anthology of Voices in the Modern American Short Story* (New York: Simon & Schuster, 1986), 312–13.

2. Paul Greenberg, "Me, Ma, Franklin Lament Death of Immigration Bill," *Grand Rapids Press*, July 4, 2007, A9.

3. L. Tyerman, *The Life and Times of Rev. Samuel Wesley* (London: Simpkin, Marshall & Co., 1866), 125.

Selected Bibliography

Albom, Mitch. *Five People You Meet in Heaven*. New York: Hyperion, 2003.

Albrecht, Karl. *The Northbound Train: Finding the Purpose, Setting the Direction, Shaping the Destiny of Your Organization*. New York: American Management Association, 1994.

Appelt, Kathi. *Miss Lady Bird's Wildflowers: How a First Lady Changed America*. San Francisco: HarperCollins, 2005.

Apps, Jerry. *Every Farm Tells a Story: A Tale of Family Farm Values*. Stillwater, MN: Voyageur Press, 2005.

Atchison, Tom. *Followership: A Practical Guide to Aligning Leaders and Followers*. Ann Arbor: Health Administration Press, 2003.

Barna, George. *The Power of Vision*. Ventura, CA: Regal, 2003.

Barna, George, ed. *Leaders on Leadership: Wisdom, Advice, and Encouragement on the Art of Leading God's People*. Ventura, CA: Regal, 1997.

Bennis, Warren G. *On Becoming a Leader*. Rev. ed. New York: Basic Books, 2003.

Bennis, Warren, and Burt Nanus. *Leaders: The Strategies for Taking Charge*. 2nd rev. ed. New York: HarperCollins, 1997.

Blanchard, Kenneth, and Sheldon Bowles. *High Five!* New York: HarperCollins, 2001.

Blanchard, Kenneth, and Spencer Johnson. *The One Minute Manager*. New York: William Morrow, 1982.

Brafman, Ori, and Rod A. Beckstrom. *The Starfish and the Spider: The Unstoppable Power of Leaderless Organizations*. New York: Portfolio, 2006.

Brookhiser, Richard. *George Washington on Leadership*. New York: Basic Books, 2008.

Burns, James MacGregor. *Leadership*. New York: HarperCollins, 1979.

Carnegie, Dale. *How to Win Friends and Influence People*. New York: Pocket, 1998.

———. *Lincoln the Unknown*. Garden City, New York: Dale Carnegie Associates, 1959.

Chaleff, Ira. *Courageous Follower: Standing Up to and for Our Leaders*. San Francisco: Berrett-Koehler, 2003.

Collins, Jim. *Good to Great: Why Some Companies Make the Leap . . . and Others Don't*. New York: Collins Business, 2001.

Covey, Stephen R. *The 7 Habits of Highly Effective People*. New York: Simon & Schuster, 1989.

Buzzell, Sid, gen. ed. *The Leadership Bible: Leadership Principles from God's Word*. Grand Rapids: Zondervan, 1998.

DePree, Max. *Leadership Is an Art*. New York: Dell, 1990.

Elstain, Jean Bethke. *Jane Addams and the Dream of American Democracy: A Life*. New York: Basic Books, 2002.

Finzel, Hans. *The Top Ten Mistakes Leaders Make*. Colorado Springs: David C. Cook, 2007.

Folsom, Burton W. *The Myth of the Robber Barons*. Herndon, VA: Young America Foundation, 1987.

Frankl, Viktor E. *Man's Search for Meaning*. New York: Simon & Schuster, 1963.

Gaines, Ernest J. *A Lesson Before Dying*. New York: Random House, 1993.

Gladwell, Malcolm. *Blink: The Power of Thinking Without Thinking*. New York: Back Bay Books, 2007.

Goethais, George R., et al. *Encyclopedia of Leadership*. New York: Sage Publications, 2004.

Goldberg, Steven. *Why Men Rule: A Theory of Male Dominance.* Chicago: Open Court, 1999.

Goleman, Daniel, et al. *Primal Leadership: Realizing the Power of Emotional Intelligence.* Boston: Harvard Business School, 2002.

Greenleaf, Robert. *Servant Leadership: A Journey into the Nature of Legitimate Power and Greatness.* New York: Paulist Press, 1977.

Grzelakowski, Moe. *Mother Leads Best: 50 Women Who Are Changing the Way Organizations Define Leadership.* New York: Kaplan Business, 2005.

Heifetz, Ronald A. *Leadership Without Easy Answers.* Boston: Harvard Business School, 1994.

Heifetz, Ronald A., and Marty Linsky. *Leadership on the Line: Staying Alive through the Dangers of Leading.* Boston: Harvard Business School, 2002.

Howes, Ruth H., and Michael Stephenson. *Women and the Use of Military Force.* Boulder, CO: Lynne Reinner Publishers, 1993.

Iacocca, Lee. *Where Have All the Leaders Gone?* New York: Scribner, 2008.

Johnson, Samuel. *Adventurer and Idler.* London: William Pickering, 1725.

Kallir, Jane. *Grandma Moses in the 21st Century.* New Haven: Yale University, 2001.

Kellerman, Barbara. *Bad Leadership: What It Is, How It Happens, Why It Matters.* Boston: Harvard Business School, 2004.

———. *Followership: How Followers Are Creating Change and Changing Leaders.* Boston: Harvard Business School, 2008.

Kelly, Robert. *The Power of Followership.* New York: Doubleday Business, 1992.

Kotter, John P. *Leading Change.* Boston: Harvard Business School, 1996.

Kouzes, James M., and Barry Z. Posner. *The Leadership Challenge.* 4th ed. San Francisco: Jossey-Bass, 2008.

Lewis, C. S. *Surprised by Joy.* New York: Harvest Books, 1966.

Lischer, Richard. *The Preacher King: Martin Luther King Jr. and the Word That Moved America*. New York: Oxford University Press, 1995.

Lowe, Janet C. *Warren Buffett Speaks: Wit and Wisdom from the World's Greatest Investor*. John Wiley & Sons, 1997.

Maxwell, John. *Developing the Leader Within You*. Nashville: Thomas Nelson, 2005.

_____. *Leadership Gold: Lessons I've Learned from a Lifetime of Leading*. Nashville: Thomas Nelson, 2008.

_____. *The 21 Indispensable Qualities of a Leader: Becoming the Person Others Will Want to Follow*. Nashville: Thomas Nelson, 2007.

McCall, Morgan W. *High Flyers: Developing the Next Generation of Leaders*. Boston: Harvard Business School, 1997.

Miller, Calvin. *The Empowered Leader: 10 Keys to Servant Leadership*. Nashville: B&H Publishing, 1997.

Moses, Anna Mary Robertson. *My Life's History*. New York: Harper-Collins, 1952.

Pausch, Randy, and Jeffrey Zaslow. *The Last Lecture*. New York: Hyperion, 2008.

Palmer, Parker. *The Courage to Teach: Exploring the Inner Landscape of a Teacher's Life*. San Francisco: Jossey-Bass, 1998.

Phillips, Donald T. *Lincoln on Leadership: Executive Strategies for Tough Times*. New York: Warner Books, 1992.

Pressman, Steven. *Outrageous Betrayal: The Dark Journey of Werner Erhard from est to Exile*. New York: St. Martin's Press, 1993.

Robinson, Marilyn. *Gilead*. New York: Farrar, Straus, and Giroux, 2004.

Redsand, Anna. *Viktor Frankl: A Life Worth Living*. New York: Clarion Books, 2006.

Riggio, Ronald E., et al. *The Art of Followership: How Great Followers Create Great Leaders and Organizations*. San Francisco: Jossey-Bass, 2008.

Rubenzer, Steven J., and Thomas R. Faschingbauer. *Personality, Character, and Leadership in the White House*. Washington DC: Potomac Books, 2004.

Sapinsley, Barbara. *The Private War of Mrs. Packard.* New York: Kodansha, 1995.

Schaef, Anne Wilson. *Women's Reality: An Emerging Female System in a White Male Society.* New York: HarperOne, 1992.

Sullivan, John J. *Servant First! Leadership for the New Millennium.* N.p.: Xulon Press, 2003.

Tapscott, Don, and Anthony D. Williams. *Wikinomics: How Mass Collaboration Changes Everything.* New York: Portfolio, 2008.

Walters, Ronald W., and Cedrick Johnson. *Bibliography of African American Leadership: An Annotated Guide.* Westport, CN: Greenwood Press, 2000.

Westhues, Kenneth. *The Envy of Excellence: Administrative Mobbing of High-Achieving Professors.* Lewiston, NY: Edwin Mellen Press, 2006.

Wheatley, Margaret J. *Leadership and the New Science: Discovering Order in a Chaotic World.* 3rd ed. San Francisco: Berrett-Koehler, 2006.

Wills, Garry. *Certain Trumpets: The Nature of Leadership.* New York: Simon & Schuster, 1994.

Woolfe, Lorin. *The Bible on Leadership: From Moses to Matthew—Management Lessons for Contemporary Leaders.* New York: AMACOM, 2002.

Veblen, Thorstein. *The Theory of the Leisure Class* (Oxford Classic). New York: Oxford University Press, 2008.

Yancey, Philip. *Soul Survivor: How My Faith Survived the Church.* New York: Doubleday, 2001.

INDEX

African American philanthropy, 161
Albom, Mitch (*Five People You Meet in Heaven*), 196
Atchison, Tom, 118
Awdry, Wilbert, 49–51

Ballou, Kathryn, 77
Barna, George, 19
Belshazzar, 216
Bennis, Warren, 20, 118, 123–24, 127, 129–30
Big Dog Leadership, 33–34
"Big Five" scale, 99–100
Blanchard, Kenneth, 19, 60
Bonhoeffer, Dietrich, 216
Brafman, Ori, and Rod A. Beckstrom (*The Starfish and the Spider*), 138–39
Brown, Willie, 28
Brunner, Emil, 109
Buffett, Warren, 40–44
Burns, James McGregor, 19
Bush, George H. W., 123–24
Bush, George W., 55–56, 81
Buzzell, Sid, 60
Byfield, Bruce, 31–33, 35

Caison, Monica, 169–71
capitalism, competitive, 43–44
carbon footprint, 175–76
Carey, Archibald, 89
Carlyle, Thomas (*On Heroes, Hero-Worship, and the Heroic in History*), 21, 85
Carnegie, Dale (*How to Win Friends and Influence People*), 31, 96–98
Carnegie, Dale (*Lincoln the Unknown*), 102
Carson, D. A., 66
Cawthon, David, 82
Chaleff, Ira, 119–20
Chamberlain, Ian, 83–84
Chanakya (Kautilya) *Arthashastra*, 71
chaos, in management theory, 135–36
character, 100–101
Character Ethic, 95
Christian Reformed Church, 28
Church, Tara, 177–78
churches, green, 180–82
Churchill, Winston, 83–84
Clark, Don, 34–35
Cloninger, Kathy, 114–15

Cohen, Octavus Roy, "Mothers' Day," 200–202
Cole, David, 94
Collins, Jim (*Good to Great*), 93–94
Collison, Jim, 113–14
complementarian (gender roles), 119
Conger, Jay, 31
conspicuous consumption, 41
contingency theory, 21
Covey, Stephen, 96
Covey, Stephen (*The 7 Habits of Highly Effective People*), 112
Cronkite, Walter, 95

Daniel, 216
David as leader, King, 23, 64
Davis, Jefferson, 211
decentralization in religion, 139–40
DeVos, Richard, 60
Drucker, Peter, 19, 118

epitaphs, 210–14
Erhard, Werner, 127–29
everyday life management, 147–48, 151

Feuerstein, Aaron, 75–77
Field, Richard, 20
followers, 118–19, 123–27, 134
  vs. leaders, 122
followership, 119–21, 124
Folsom, Burton W. (*The Myth of the Robber Barons*), 41
Forbes, Malcolm, 19
Frankl, Viktor, 171–73

Gaines, Ernest J. (*A Lesson Before Dying*), 155–58, 160
gender
  language, impact of, 110–11
  roles/differences, 106–7
Girl Scouts, 114–15
Goldberg, Steven (*Why Men Rule*), 112–13
Grandma Moses (Anna Mary Robertson), 199–200
"Great Man" theory, 10–11, 21, 63, 80–86, 90, 102

Greenleaf, Robert K., 73
Greenleaf, Robert K. (*Servant Leadership*), 77

Hamilton, Alexander, 210
Harari, Eli, 95
headship, biblical, 108–9
Heathfield, Susan, 32–33
Heifetz, Ronald, 53, 56, 89
Heifetz, Ronald (*Leadership on the Line*), 19
Heifetz, Ronald (*Leadership without Easy Answers*), 85
Hess, Rudolf, 51–52
Hesse, Herman (*The Journey to the East*), 74–75
Hitler, Adolf, 51–53
Howes, Ruth and Michael Stevenson, 112
humor, impact on memory, 187–88
Hunt, Darryl, 168–69

Iacocca, Lee (*Iacocca*), 93–94
Iacocca, Lee (*Where Have All the Leaders Gone?*), 55

Jefferson, Thomas, 154–56, 158–59, 161, 210–11
Jesus as leadership model, 69–72
Johnson, Lady Bird, 183–84
Joseph as leader, 64

Keillor, Garrison, 191–93
Kellerman, Barbara, 54–55, 133–34
Kelley, Robert (*The Power of Followership*), 120
Kennedy, John F., 95
King, Martin Luther, 23, 86–87, 89–92, 211
King, Mike, 87–89
Kinsley, Michael, 30–31, 135

leaderlessness, postmodern science of, 135
leadership
  American vs. African styles, 44–46
  bad, 51, 53–55

bad vs. good, 57–58
biblical, evaluation of, 59–68
business of, 30–31
cult of, 31–32, 34–35
Christian, subjectivity of, 19–20, 64
decentralization of, 135–39
defining, 18–20, 24–25, 115, 215
early church, in, 66–67
four theories of, 21–22
gender differences, 107–8, 112–13, 119
globalization, impact of, 22
Internet, impact of, 132–33
Jesus, philosophy of, 62–63
Katrina as disaster of, 136
made or born, 29–30
vs. management, 20–21
Pauline perspective, 66–67
personality, identifying the, 94–95
qualifications questioned, 17–18
science of, 134–35
sixteen types of (Gary Wills), 22–23
and success, 66
transparency, 42–43
twenty cells of (Carter McNamara), 23–24
women in, 107–9
Lead Well, 132
Leadership Bible, The, 60–64
Leadership Cube, 24
Leadership IQ, 35–36
Left Behind in a Megachurch World, 186
legacy, 11, 30, 92, 115, 143–53, 215–16
environmental, creating an, 174–84
faith, role of, 152–53
family/friends, role of, 151–52
humor, role of, 185–94
mortality's role in, 205–14
tender mercies, creating, 195–204
wealth, role of, 160–61
"left-behind" mentality, developing a, 206
legacy footprint, 12, 216
Leo, 74–75
Lewis, C. S., 198–99
Lincoln, Abraham, 89–90, 102–4
Low, Juliette Gordon, 114
Luther, Martin, 65–66

management, science of, 136
MacDonald, Gordon, 68
McKinsey management consulting, 30, 135
McNamara, Carter, 23–24
Maxwell, John, 19, 60, 119
Maxwell Leadership Bible, The, 61
Mind Tools, 37–38
mobbing, 124–25
Moses as leader, 63–64
Mother Teresa as leader, 69–70, 73

Napoleon, 23
negotiation, 112
Nehemiah as leader, 64
New Age, 139–40
noncompetitive system, female, 47–48

"objectivist myth," 16
Oprah, 158, 160–61

Packard, Theophilus and Elizabeth, 164–68
Palmer, Parker (The Courage to Teach), 16–17, 46
Paul, Apostle
as leader, 64–65, 68
view of women, 108–9
Peale, Norman Vincent (The Power of Positive Thinking), 96
Personality Ethic, 95–96
Peterson, Eugene, 126
Phillips, Donald T. (Lincoln on Leadership), 103
Piper, John, 105–6
positive mental attitude (PMA), 96
presidents as leaders, 98–99
Putin, Vladimir, 9–11
pyramid leadership, contemporary, 67

Quakers (Society of Friends), 78

Reagan, Ronald, 81, 123–24
recycling, 179
robber barons, 41
Robinson, Marilynne (Gilead), 198
Romney, Mitt, 30

Roosevelt, Eleanor, 23
Roosevelt, Franklin, 23
Rowling, J. K., 115–16
Rubenzer, Steven and Thomas Faschingbauer (*Personality, Character, and Leadership in the White House*), 98–99

Schael, Anne Wilson (*Women's Reality*), 46
scientific management, 135
servant leadership, 69–79
shared leadership, 66–67
situationist theory, 21, 86
Socrates, 23
Spencer, Herbert, 21
Stevenson, Adlai, 23
swarm theory, 137–38

Tanner, Roy, 77
Taylor, Frederick Winslow, 135
transactional theory, 22
Tripp, Dick, 66
Truman, Harry, 57
Truth, Sojourner, 111–12
Tubman, Harriet, 23

Van Atta, Dale, 53
Veblen, Thorstein (*The Theory of the Leisure Class*), 41
vision, 34–35

Webster, Noah, 25–26
Wenceslas, Good King, 71–72
Wesley, John, 213–14
Wesley, Charles, 212
Wesley, Susanna, 211–13
Westhues, Kenneth (*The Envy of Excellence*), 124
Wheatley, Margaret J. (*Leadership and the New Science*), 135–36
white male system, 46–47
Williams, Brian, 95
Wills, Gary, 23, 89, 122
Woolfe, Lorin (*The Bible on Leadership*), 59–60, 64
Woolman, John, as servant leader, 77–79

Yancey, Philip, 92

Zaleznik, Abraham, 20
Zondervan, 60–61

Ruth A. Tucker, Ph.D. served for twenty-five years as a professor at Trinity Evangelical Divinity School and Calvin Theological Seminary. She is the author of seventeen books, including *Walking Away from Faith* and her Gold Medallion award-winning *From Jerusalem to Irian Jaya*. She makes her home in Grand Rapids, Michigan, with her husband, John Worst, professor of music emeritus at Calvin College. They have a blended family of three children and four grandchildren.